VOLUME II OF THE OCCULT MANUALS
TRUE OCCULT KNOWLEDGE GIVES YOU
PRACTICAL POWER AND STRENGTH

THE
ASTRAL WORLD

ITS SCENES, DWELLERS, AND PHENOMENA

BY
SWAMI PANCHADASI

Published 2000
The Book Tree
Escondido, CA

ADVANCED THOUGHT PUBLISHING CO.
168 N. MICHIGAN AVE., CHICAGO, ILL.

The Astral World
ISBN 1-58509-071-9

©2000
THE BOOK TREE
All Rights Reserved

INTRODUCTION

Most books that cover the astral realms are written by westerners who have had some interesting experiences, but lack the overall knowledge of an Indian spiritual master. Swami Panchadasi was such a master. He has written an incredible classic that covers all aspects of the astral world and reveals much of what is missing from the traditional western perspective.

We often wonder if there are other worlds or other realities. Panchadasi assures us that there are, and goes into vivid detail as to what these other realities are composed of and how we can access them. However, he starts off with the basics, covering the entire "lay of the land" or composition of this new reality, before bringing us further in.

This is a great book for curious beginners and serious seekers alike, as it is structured to go gradually from simple to advanced information within the span of 100 pages. The author clearly writes from first hand experience, revealing important information that one would otherwise have to scour through dozens of volumes to find.

Traveling into the unknown can be a frightening experience, but Panchadasi prepares the reader well. Instead of ignoring possible pitfalls, he provides warnings when necessary, which many readers will be grateful for. The astral world is quite different from the physical one, replete with strange, uncharted territory and actual forms of consciousness that can be intelligent, beautiful, helpful, and loving, but sometimes malicious and dangerous. Swami Panchadasi has been there and returned, providing a very useful map in the form of this book. By either following the map and engaging in astral travel, or simply reading this book as an interested "bystander," one can be assured of having a rewarding experience.

Paul Tice

CONTENTS

CHAPTER I.

THE SEVEN PLANES.

EVERY student of occultism, from the humblest beginner to the most advanced pupil, has a full realization of the wonders of that strange plane of being known as The Astral World. The beginner, of course, has not the privilege of actually viewing life on this plane, except, perhaps, in exceptional cases, or under extraordinary circumstances. But even he finds constant reference to the subject in the treatise his studies, and soon discovers that that particular plane is the scene and field of some very strange phenomena.

As he advances, and learns more of the occult laws and principles, he develops still greater interest in the subject. And, when he reaches the stage in which he is able to actually sense (by astral vision) on this plane, he finds that a new world of experience has opened out before him.

The oldest occult teachings, as well as the latest, inform the student that there are Seven Planes of Being. The lowest of these planes is that which is known as the Material Plane.

Second in order is that which is known as the Plane of Forces. The third is that which is known as the Astral Plane. The fourth is that which is known as the Mental Plane.

Above these four planes are three higher planes, known to occultists, but which have no names that can be understood by those dwelling only on the lower planes, and which are incapable of explanation to those on the lower planes. I shall refer to some of these higher planes, in this little book, as we proceed, but shall make no attempt to describe them for the reasons just given. Our subject for the present consideration is merely the Astral Plane, and we shall find sufficient interesting facts in considering the phenomena of that plane without attempting to penetrate the veils of those still higher.

It should be mentioned at this point, that each of the Seven Planes has seven sub-planes; and that each of these sub-planes has its own seven subdivisions; and so on to the seventh degree of subdivision. So, you see, there is a most minute classification in the occult teachings.

The student of occultism, at the beginning, usually experiences difficulty in forming a clear conception of the meaning of the word "plane" as used in the occult teachings. Consulting the dictionary, he is apt to get the idea of a plane as one of a series of straight layers— one part of a great strata—above and below which are other layers or strata. It usually is quite difficult for the occult teacher to eradicate this erroneous idea from the mind of his pupils, and to substitute the correct concept.

This error arises from thinking of these planes of being as composed of matter, or material substance, which, of course, is incorrect. When it is remembered that even the densest form of matter itself is composed of vibrations of energy (as recognized by modern science), and that the Forces of Nature are but manifestations of vibrations of energy, one begins to find the key. Instead of the planes rising one above the other in the scale of the fineness of matter, they are graded according to their respective degrees of vibration of energy. In short, they are planes of vibrations of energy, and not planes of matter at all. Matter is simply the lowest degree of vibrations of energy, that is all.

The second common source of error, on the part of the beginner in occultism, is that of picturing the planes as lying one above the other in space. This conception, of course, naturally follows upon the error of thinking of the planes as a series of layers or strata of fine matter; but it also often persists even after the student has grasped the idea that the planes are grades of vibration, rather than of matter. But, finally, the student is impressed with the idea that the planes are not "layers" or "strata" at all. The planes do not lie one above the other, in space. They have not spatial distinction or degree. They interpenetrate each other in the same point of space. A single point of space may have its manifestations of each and all of the seven planes of being.

Some of the old occultists sought to explain this condition of things to their students in the words of a very celebrated ancient teacher, who originated the aphorism: "A plane of being is not a place, but a state of being." No words can give a better explanation of, or aid, to, the correct mental conception of the idea of a "plane" in the occult sense of the term.

To those students who may find it difficult to form the idea of a number of manifestations, each having its own rate of vibration, occupying the same point of space at the same time, I would say that a little consideration of the phenomena of the physical world will perhaps serve as an aid in the matter. For instance, every student of physics knows that a single point of space may contain vibrations of heat, light of many shades, magnetism, electricity, X rays, etc., etc., each manifesting its own rate of vibration, and yet not interfering with the others.

Every beam of sunlight contains many different colors, each with its own rate of vibration, and yet none crowding out the others. By the proper laboratory apparatus each kind of light may be separated from the others, and the ray thus split up. The difference in the colors arise simply from the different rate of etheric vibrations.

Again it is possible to send many telegrams along the same wire, at the same time, by using senders and receivers of different vibratory "keynotes." The same thing has its corresponding analogy in the case of wireless telegraphy. So, you see, even on the physical planes we find many forms of vibratory manifestation occupying the same point of space at the same time.

The Material Plane, with which we are all familiar, has, of course, its seven sub-planes, and likewise its seven-times-seven series of subdivisions, as have all the seven planes. At first we are apt to think that we are perfectly familiar with every form of matter, but this is far from being the case, for we are familiar with only a few forms. The occult teachings show us that on certain of the fixed stars, and some of the planets of our own chain, there are forms and kinds of matter as much lower in vibration than the densest form of matter known to us, as these dense forms are lower than the highest ultra-gaseous forms of matter recognized by us. And, on the other hand, the same teachings inform us that there are in existence,, in other worlds, and even (to an extent) in our own, forms and kinds of matter as much higher than these highest forms of ultra-gaseous matter known to us, as the said known forms are higher than the densest form of matter now known to us. This is a startling statement, but every advanced occultist knows it to be true.

Physical science formerly classified matter as follows: (1) solids; (2) liquids; (3) gaseous. But modern science has found many forms of matter far more tenuous and rarer than even the finest gas. It now calls this fourth class "ultra-gaseous matter." But occultists know that beyond this fourth sub-plane of matter which science is just now discovering, there lie three other, and still finer, sub-planes, of which science at present has no conception.

Next higher in the scale of manifested being, we find what is known as the Plane of Forces, of which very little is known outside of occult science, although, of later years, physical science has been breaking into this field. In the next twenty years physical science will proceed further in this direction. The research into radio-activity is leading toward further knowledge regarding this plane of manifestation.

On the Plane of Forces, we find the seven sub-planes, and likewise the seven-times-seven subdivision. There are forces far below the scale of the ordinary forces of Nature known to man. And, likewise, there are great series of Nature's Finer Forces at the other end of the scale, of which the ordinary man—even the scientist—knows nothing. It is these finer forces which account for many of the wonders of occult science. In particular, the fine force called "prana" or "vital force," plays an important part in all occult phenomena.

Next above the scale of the Plane of Forces, we find the great Astral Plane, the consideration of which is the purpose of this little book.

CHAPTER II.

ASTRAL REGIONS.

IN the occult teachings we find frequent references to what are called "the astral regions," and the inhabitants and phenomena of said regions. Like the term "plane," this term "region" has caused much misunderstanding. The old occultists used it in a loose sense, knowing that their pupils clearly understood the real significance. They did not care whether or not other persons understood. But the modern investigator, without the benefit of a teacher, often finds himself confused by this mention of "regions" of the Astral Plane, and frequently finds himself thinking of them in the sense of the "heavens and hells" of the old theology—as definite places in space. But these astral regions are nothing more than vibrational manifestations on the Astral Plane, which have no special reference to any set-aside portion of space, and which manifestations may, and do, occur at almost any point of space. The astral regions occupy the same space as the material regions, neither interfering with the other.

The term "astral" is derived from the Greek

word meaning "related to a star," and was originally used in describing the heavens of the Greeks—the abodes of their gods. From this sense and usage the term widened in application, until it was employed to indicate what might be called the "ghostland" of the ancient people. This ghostland was believed to be inhabited by beings of an etheral nature, not only disembodied spirits, but also angelic beings of a higher order.

The ancient occultists of Greece, and other Western lands, thus naturally fell into the custom of using the familiar term to indicate that which we know as the Astral Plane in modern occultism. Of course, the Oriental occultists had their own terms for this plane of manifestation, which terms were derived from old Sanscrit roots, and which were much older than the Greek terms. But, as the use of Sanscrit terms has a tendency to confuse Western students, the best Oriental teachers, today, in teaching Western students, almost always use the old Greek occult terms.

At this point, I must answer a question which usually presents itself to the mind of the intelligent student at about this particular stage of the teaching. It is probably in the mind of the student who is reading these words, at this particular moment. The question may be stated as follows: "How is it possible for anyone to speak intelligently of the phenomena of the Astral Plane, if that plane is on a higher vibratory scale than the physical senses. How can one visit, and perceive things on, the Astral Plane, without his body being dematerialized?"

This question is a natural and perfectly fair one, and evidences the inquiring mind which the true occultist always possesses. And no true occult teacher will hesitate for a moment in frankly answering it. For, remember this always, my students, the occult teaching is not based merely on the principles laid down as "gospel" by the old occultists. Respect, yes! great respect is paid to these old teachings, of course, but every advanced occultist knows that he must actually experience the manifestation of occult phenomena before he can positively pronounce the same to be an occult truth. Such experience comes to every advanced occultist, when he reaches the necessary stage of development which alone renders such experience safe for him. Like the scientist, the true occultist learns by his own experience, built upon the recorded previous experience of others. To the advanced occultist the phenomena of the Astral Plane is just as real—just as readily sensed—as is the phenomena of the material plane to those functioning upon it.

But, to answer the question: One does not have to disintegrate or dematerialize his physical body in order to visit or sense the Astral Plane and its phenomena. There are two avenues of approach to the Astral Plane, as follows: (1) by the employment of the astral senses; and (2) by visiting in the so-called "astral body." Let us consider each of these avenues in turn.

By the term "the astral senses," occultists indicate that wonderful secondary set of senses, corresponding in office to the five physical senses, by means of which man is able to receive impressions on the Astral Plane.

Each of the physical senses of man has its astral counterpart, which functions on the astral plane just as the physical senses do upon the material plane. Thus every man has, in latency, the power of seeing, hearing, feeling, smelling, and tasting, on the astral plane, by means of these five astral senses. Nay more, as all advanced occultists know, man really has seven physical senses instead of five, though these additional two senses are not sufficiently developed for use in the average person (though the occultist of fair attainment generally unfolds them into use). And even these two extra physical senses also have their astral counterparts.

In the cases of persons who, accidentally or through careful training, have developed the power of astral vision—perception through astral sight—the scenes of the Astral Plane are perceived just as clearly as are those of the material plane perceived by the physical sense of sight. The ordinary clairvoyant has flashes of this astral vision, as a rule, and is not able to sense astrally by an act of will. The trained occultist, on the other hand, is able to shift from one set of senses to another, by an act of will, whenever he wishes to do so. In fact, such occultists may function on both planes at the same time, in this way, if they so desire.

In cases of clairvoyance, or astral visioning, the occultist remains in his physical body, and senses the phenomena of the Astral Plane quite naturally or easily. It is not necessary for him even to enter into a trance condition, or any abnormal mental state or condition. And still less is it necessary for him to leave his physical body in such cases. In the instance of the higher form of clairvoyance, he may even sense events both on the physical plane, as well as the astral planes, at a distance— though, strictly speaking, this belongs to a somewhat different order of occult phenomena. To vision astrally, the occultist has merely to shift his sensory mechanism, just as the operator on the typewriter shifts from the small letter type to the capitals by a shiftkey. This, then, is the simplest and most common way of occult sensing on the Astral Plane. It is possible to many to whom the second method is impossible.

The second avenue of approach to the Astral Plane is that in which the individual leaves his physical body, and actually travels on the Astral Plane in his astral body. The astral body is composed of an etheral substance of a very high degree of vibration. It is not mere matter, and yet is not mere force—it is composed of astral substance which resembles very fine matter, but which is far more tenuous than anything that is known as matter. Ordinarily the astral body can be sensed only by means of the astral vision, but under certain other conditions it takes on the semblance of a vapory form of matter, and is perceptible to the ordinary physical senses as a "ghost" or "apparition," even when the person is in physical life.

The astral body is an exact counterpart of the physical body, but survives the latter by a number of years. It is not immortal, however, and finally disintegrates and is resolved into its original elements just as is the physical body.

The advanced occultist, in his astral body, is able to leave his physical body (which remains in a state of sleep or trance) and to visit at will on the Astral Plane, even at points in space far removed from his physical body.

He, however, is always connected with the physical body by a thin, cobweb-like, filament of ethereal substance, which extends or contracts as he travels away from, or toward, the sleeping physical body. If this filament is broken by an accident on the Astral Plane, his physical body "dies" and he is never able to return to it. Such accidents are rare, but occult history has records showing their occasional occurrence.

Many persons are able to travel in the astral body, during ordinary sleep, but usually have no recollection of the same upon reawakening. The occultist, on the other hand, travels consciously, and with a purpose, and always is wide-awake on such journeys. He is as much at home on the Astral Plane as on the physical one.

And so, student, you see how the occult teaching regarding the Astral Plane has been obtained; and how such teaching has as firm a basis in actual experience as have those based upon physical observation, experiment, and experience. Moreover, every occultist may verify the teaching for himself—in fact actually does so.

CHAPTER III.

REALITY OF THE ASTRAL.

IT is customary among occultists to speak of the Astral Plane, simply as "the Astral," as for instance "out in the Astral;" "visiting the Astral;" "phenomena of the Astral;" "inhabitants of the Astral," etc., etc. The student may as well familiarize himself with this use of the term "the Astral," in order to understand, and be understood by, others interested in occult study. Accordingly, I shall from now on use this term, "the Astral," as indicating the Astral Regions—the Astral Plane—without further explanation.

One of the hardest things for the elementary student to realize is that the Astral is just as real, abiding, and fixed as is the material world. Just as steam is actually as real as water, or even as ice, so is the Astral just as real as the world of the physical senses. For that matter, if we could see our world of matter placed under a sufficiently strong magnifying glass, we should perceive it not as a great body of solid fixed matter, but rather as an aggregation of an infinite number of the tiniest particles themselves built into atoms; these built into molecules; and these built into solid masses.

The space between the ions of the material atom is as comparatively great as the space between the planets of our solar system. And every ion, atom and molecule is in constant and intense motion. Under a glass of sufficient power, there would seem to be nothing solid in the material world. If the magnifying glass were to be raised to an infinite power, even the ions would melt into seething nothingness, and there would be nothing left but the ether which has no weight and which is imperceptible to the senses even when aided by the strongest instruments of the laboratory. So you see, the solidity of things is merely relative and comparative. The vibration of substance on the Astral is higher than those of the material plane; but even the Astral vibrations are far slower than those of the next higher plane, and so on.

To the traveller on the Astral the scenery, and everything connected therewith, seems as solid as the most solid material does to the physical eye. It really is just as solid as is the astral body in which you visit it, for that matter. As for reality, the Astral is just as real as is the material, in every respect.

The Forces of Nature are not perceptible to the physical eye, except as manifesting through matter—but they are very real as all of us know by experience. You cannot see electricity, but when you receive its shock you realize its reality. You cannot see the force of gravity, but you become painfully aware of its reality when it drops an apple on your head; or causes you to fall suddenly when you make a misstep on the curb of the street. In fact, it is realized by all advanced occultists, that if there really can be said to be any degrees in reality between things, the balance is in favor of the finer forms of substance and forces, and against the less fine.

So, student, never permit yourself to think of the Astral as something comparatively unreal, or as only relatively existent. I, of course, am not speaking of Reality in the metaphysical sense of the term, for in such sense the entire manifested universe, including all of its planes, is unreal as compared to the One Reality. And, again, do not permit yourself to think of the astral senses as being one whit less real, reliable and important than those of the physical body. Each class of sense perception has its own proper field in which it is king. Each is master in its own realm. And there should be no attempt to draw distinctions of reality between them. At the last, they are all but the mechanism of consciousness, or "awareness," each adapted to the peculiar requirements of its environment.

The Astral has its scenery, geography (!), and "things," just as has the material world. These things are just as real as are England, the Vatican, St. Paul's, the Capitol at Washington; Broadway, Picadilly, or the Rue de la Paix; the Great Redwood Trees of California, the Grand Canyon, the Alps, or the Black Forest. Its inhabitants are just as real as any of the great men of the country in which you live, or those of any other country, whose names I hesitate to call, lest they pass from this material plane and thus become "unreal" even before these printed words pass before your eye, so impermanent are the inhabitants and things of even this real (!) material world.

The law of constant change operates on the Astral just as on the material plane. There, things come and go, just as they do here on the material plane. Stop a moment and concentrate on the gist of the matter, and you will see that the difference between the things of the two planes is simply like the difference between red and blue—simply a difference in the rate of vibration of substance. And, this again, is the cause of the difference between steel and hydrogen gas, between electricity and light, between magnetism and heat—simply a difference of vibrations of substance.

Moreover, and this is quite important to the student, the Astral has its laws just as has the material world. These laws must be learned and observed, otherwise the inhabitants of the Astral, as well as the visitor thereto, will reap the result which always comes from broken natural laws.

Again, there exists what may be called the "geography" of the Astral, if this material-plane word is permitted in this connection. There are regions, points of space, places, kingdoms, countries, etc., on the Astral, just as on the material plane. Sometimes these Astral regions have no connection with any on the material plane, while in other cases they have a very direct connection with and relation to, material places and the inhabitants thereof.

One may travel from one region of the Astral to another, by simply an act of will which raises the vibration of the astral body, without it moving a point in space. Again, one may travel in space from one point to another on the Astral, in cases where these points have some relation to points on the material plane.

As an instance of this latter form of travel, I would say that one may travel in the Astral from Berlin to Bombay—in but the twinkle of an eye, as regards time,—by merely wishing or willing to do so. Yes! time and space have their manifestation on the Astral. But, nevertheless, certain Astral manifestations, on its seven-times-seven sub-planes, may be, and likely are, present THERE in, at, and on, the exact point of space which you are occupying at this moment on the material plane—and this very moment of time, NOW!

If you have the knowledge and power, you, without leaving your seat, may traverse all of these sub-planes, one after the other, witnessing their scenery and inhabitants, their phenomena and activity, and then return to the material plane—all in a moment of time, and without changing a single point in space.

Or, if you prefer, you may travel to any of these sub-planes of the Astral, at your point of space, and then travel in space on the Astral to some other place on that sub-plane; and then have the choice of returning either the same way by which you came, or else descending to the material plane and travelling on it,

in your astral body, back to where your
physical body is resting. Read over these last
two paragraphs, until you get the idea clearly
fixed in your mind, for by so doing you will
be able to comprehend more easily that which
I shall have to say to you in the following
chapters of this book.

In travelling on the Astral, one meets with
many strange inhabitants of that wonderful
realm of Nature—some pleasant and others
unpleasant. Some of these inhabitants have
passed on from the material plane, while others
have never dwelt there, these latter forms
being natives of the Astral and peculiar to
itself.

In my personal class instruction, I have
found it advantageous to my students for me
to describe the phenomena of the Astral to
them in my lectures, in the form of the story
of a trip in the Astral, rather than as a dry,
technical description. In such lectures, I
assume that the students are present on the
Astral with me, and that I am acting as their
guide. In this way, a much clearer conception
of the subject seems to be gained by them.
After careful consideration, I have decided to
follow this same plan—in part, at least—in
some of the following chapters. I need scarcely

add that the descriptions given are based upon the actual experiences of advanced occultists, including myself, and are not dogmatic statements of theory, conjectures, or speculations of mere "book occultists." Every fact herein stated may be verified by the experience of any advanced occultist.

CHAPTER IV.

PASSING THE BORDER.

I DO not deem it advisable to enter into a description of the technical details attend-ant upon the process of passing out of the physical body into the astral body of finer substance. Any description of this kind, even though it be but merely a suggestion of the facts, might give an untrained person at least a hint of the process, which might lead him to experiment, and which might bring upon him very undesirable results. I shall pass over this stage, for the reasons stated, which will meet with the approval of every advanced occultist and careful student of occultism. * * *

Now, student, you find yourself outside of your physical form or body, and clad in your astral form alone. You probably think that I am joking with you, for as you glance at your body you find that it appears not different from your ordinary one. Even your clothing is the same, to the most minute detail—this occurs through perfectly natural laws on the Astral plane, which I cannot take time to explain at this time.

out of the physical body, when you turn your head and perceive your own physical form, as well as mine, seemingly sunk in sleep in the arm chairs in which we seated ourselves a few moments ago.

Looking a little closer, you will see that your astral form, as well as mine, is connected with its physical counterpart by a tiny, thin, tenuous filament of ethereal substance, resembling a rope of shining spider-web silk. This filament is capable of expansion, and contraction, and enables you to move about freely.

Now concentrate your attention as you have been taught to do, 'and will that your vibrations increase in rate, but in perfect harmony with mine, so that you will keep in my company instead of moving on to other sub-planes or sub-visions, parting with my company. You would not find it exactly safe or pleasant to leave my presence, until you have learned to pilot yourself in these strange waters.

You will find yourself with me in a strange atmosphere, although you have not moved an inch in space. Behind you, so to speak, you perceive dimly the room in which we were just living; and ahead of you, so to speak, you perceive strange flashes and streaks of phosphorescent light of different hues and tints.

These are the vibrations and waves of force, for you are now passing through the Plane of Forces. That vivid, bluish streak is the passage of some electric current—probably a wireless message flashing through space. Back of you, on my table, you see the magnetic ore, or lodestone, paper-weight, which always lies there. But now you see the peculiar phosphorescence around its poles, which is not visible on the material plane.

You also notice a peculiar faint vibratory glow around every physical object—this is the force of atomic and molecular attraction, etc. Still fainter, you find a peculiar radiance permeating the entire atmosphere—this is the outward sign of the force of gravitation. These things are all very interesting, and if you were a learned physicist, or great physical scientist, you could scarcely be dragged from this plane, so interesting would be the study of force made visible. But, as you are not such a person, you will see more interesting sights ahead of you.

Now, you feel your life force vibrating at a higher rate, and realize that the sense of weight seems to be dropping from you. You feel as light as a feather, and feel as though you could move without an effort. Well, you may begin to walk. Yes, "walk," I said! You are still on earth, and the floor of the room is still there under your feet.

Let us walk through the wall of the room, and out into the street. Don't be afraid, step through the wall as if it were made of fog. There, you see how easy it is. Odd thing, really stepping through a brick and stone wall, isn't it? But it's still more odd when you stop to consider that as we moved the wall really passed through our thin substance, instead of the latter passing through the wall—that's the real secret of it.

Now let us walk down the street. Step out just as if you were in the flesh—stop a moment! there you let that man walk right through you! And he never even saw you! Do you realize that we are ghosts? Just as much a ghost as was Hamlet's father, except that his physical body was mouldering in the ground, while ours are asleep awaiting our return to them. There! that dog saw you. And that horse vaguely feels your presence! See how nervous he is! Animals possess very keen psychic senses, compared to those of man.

But cease thinking of yourself, and look closely at the persons passing by you. You notice that each one is surrounded by an egg-

shaped aura extending on all sides of him to
the distance of about two or three feet. Do
you notice the kaleidoscopic play of blending
colors in the aura? Notice the difference in
the shades and tints of these colors, and also
observe the predominance of special colors in
each case! You know what these colors mean,
for I have instructed you regarding them in my
teaching on "The Human Aura, and Astral
Colors."

Notice that beautiful spiritual blue around
that woman's head! And see that ugly muddy
red around that man passing her! Here comes
an intellectual giant—see that beautiful golden
yellow around his head, like a nimbus! But I
don't exactly like that shade of red around his
body—and there is too marked an absence of
blue in his aura! He lacks harmonious development.

Do you notice those great clouds of semi-
luminous substance, which are slowly floating
along?—notice how the colors vary in them.
Those are clouds of thought vibrations, repre-
senting the composite thought of a multitude
of people. Also notice how each body of
thought is drawing to itself little fragments of
similar thought forms and energy. You see
here the tendency of thought forces to attract

others of their kind—how like the proverbial birds of a feather, they flock together—how thoughts come home, bringing their friends with them—how each man creates his own thought atmosphere.

Speaking of atmospheres, do you notice that each shop we pass has its own peculiar thought atmosphere? If you look into the houses on either side of the street, you will see that the same thing is true. The very street itself has its own atmosphere, created by the composite thought of those inhabiting and frequenting it. No! do not pass down that side street—its astral atmosphere is too depressing, and its colors too horrible and disgusting for you to witness just now—you might get discouraged and fly back to your physical body for relief!

Look at those thought forms flying through the atmosphere! What a variety of form and coloring! Some most beautiful, the majority quite neutral in tint, and occasionally a fierce, fiery one tearing its way along toward its mark. Observe those whirling and swirling tiny cyclonic thought-forms as they are thrown off from that business house. Across the street, notice that great octopus monster of a thought-form, with its great tentacles striving to wind around passing persons and draw them into

that flashy dance-hall and dram-shop.   A devil-
ish monster which we would do well to destroy.
Turn your concentrated thought upon it, and
will it out of existence—there, that's the right
way; watch it sicken and shrivel!   But alas!
more of its kind will come forth from that
place.

Here, will yourself up above the level of the
housetops—you can do it easily, if you only
realize that you can—there, I have helped you
to do it this time, it's quite easy when you
once gain confidence.   However, if you lose
confidence, and grow afraid, down you will
tumble to the ground, and will bruise your
astral body.

From this height look down around you.
You will see a great multitude of tiny candle-
like lights—each represents a human soul.
Here or there you will see a few much brighter
lights, and far apart you will see some that
shine like a brilliant electric spark—these last
are the auric symbols of an advanced soul.
"Let your light so shine—"!' Behold the radiance emerging from that humble house of
religious worship, and contrast it with the
unpleasant auric atmosphere of that mag-
nificent church structure next door to it—can

you not read the story of spirituality and the lack of it in the cases of these churches?

But these sights, interesting though they be, and as useful as they are in illustrating the lessons you have learned in the class, or from the manual, are far less in the scale than those which we shall witness in a moment. Come, take my hand. Our vibrations are raising. * * * Come!

CHAPTER V.

SOME LOWER SUB-PLANES.

NOW, student, we are entering the vibrations of the lower sub-planes of the Astral. You must nerve yourself to witness some unpleasant sights, but be not afraid for nothing can harm you here while I am with you. Were you' alone here, lacking the knowledge of self-protection, you might find the experience very terrifying. But, even then, though you lacked the higher knowledge, if you would but maintain a positive mental state, and deny the power of the Astral inhabitants to harm you, you would still be safe. A firm mental attitude, and the assertion of your own immunity will act as a barrier through which these influences cannot penetrate.

Your first impression is that the material world is still around you, with all its scenes plainly visible. But, as you look you will find that there seems to be a peculiar veil between those scenes and the plane upon which you are temporarily dwelling. This veil, while at least semi-transparent, nevertheless seems to have a peculiar appearance of resistent solidity, and you find yourself instinctively realizing that it would be a barrier to the passage of the astral entities back to the material plane.

I now change our vibrations, for a moment, to those of a very unpleasant subdivision of the lowest sub-plane. This is the subdivision which the old occultists were wont to call "the Astral cemetery." We shall stay on this plane of vibrations but for a moment, for it furnishes a ghastly sight, and its atmosphere is most depressing. Now, hold tight to me, and press close up to me, for you will instinctively feel the need of protection. Gazing around you on all sides, you will see what appear to be the disintegrating forms of human beings, and even some animals. These forms seem to be floating in space. They seem real, and yet, some way, not real. You realize that they are not physical bodies, but still they bear too close a resemblance to physical corpses to be pleasant. Take one good look around you, for I shall change our vibrations in a moment. * * * There! we have left that scene behind us! But before proceeding further, we shall pause a moment and consider what we have just witnessed.

These disintegrating astral forms are what occultists know as the "astral shells." The astral shell is really an astral corpse, just as the physical body in the grave is the material corpse. For, as we shall presently see, the disembodied soul eventually leaves the Astral and moves on to what the occultists know as the mental or spiritual planes of being, which are symbolized by the race conception of "the heavens," of which all religions teach. When the soul so passes on, it leaves behind it the astral body it has inhabited while on the Astral. This astral body, or form, then begins to disintegrate, and in time disappears altogether, being resolved to its original elements. During this process, it dwells on this particular division of one of the lower subdivisions of the lowest Astral sub-plane. This particular division has no other purpose, and is separate and apart from the other subdivisions.

There is a great difference between the astral shells of different individuals, so far as is concerned the duration of the shells in this particular place of disintegration. For instance, the astral of a person of high spirituality and ideals will disintegrate very rapidly indeed, as its atoms have little or no cohesive attraction when once it is discarded. But, on the other hand, the astral shell of a person of earthly ideals and material tendencies will hold together for a comparatively long time, so strong is the attractive force generated while the shell is occupied by its owner.

Those astral bodies are "dead" and have no consciousness or intelligence, and as a rule cannot even be galvanized into appearing a life as can the class of astral forms known as the "spectres," or "shades," which belong to a slightly different category, and which we shall now glance at for a moment. * * * There! gaze on the scene for a moment, before I change the vibrations again. * * *

Our momentary glimpse of the subdivision of the Astral upon which the spectral forms abide, was not a pleasant one, but it is interesting because it explains some peculiar features of psychic or occult phenomena which is often misinterpreted. You noticed that instead of floating about in astral space, as did the shells which we saw a few moments back, these spectres acted like shadowy human beings in a dazed or dreamlike condition. You saw them walking dreamily about, without set object or purpose—a weird, unpleasant sight.

These spectres are really astral shells from which the souls have departed, but which have left in them sufficient power, arising from the former thought and will vibrations of their owners, to give them a temporary semblance of life and action. This power gradually wears away, and the shell then sinks to the subdivision which we saw a little further back. In the meantime, it dwells on this particular subdivision.

In the case of the soul with high ideals and spiritual aspirations, there are practically no material thought vibrations remaining to "galvanize" the astral body after the soul has withdrawn itself. Its higher nature has neutralized these lower, but strong, vibrations. But in the case of the soul retaining strong material thoughts and desires, the power is much stronger. In the latter class, even after the higher nature of the soul has drawn it upward, above the Astral, these lower mental vibrations may persist in the deserted astral form, and thus give to the latter a semblance of life and activity which, though a counterfeit, may manifest considerable power for a time.

The counterfeit power of these spectral forms steadily decreases, but in some cases it persists for a comparatively long time. As a rule, the power disappears in the way stated, but in certain other cases it is used up, as a spark is rendered bright by blowing upon it, by means of a psychic stimulus from persons

living on the material plane. I am now allud-
ing to the power generated in "circles," and
through mediumistic persons, on the material
plane or earth life. The psychic power so
generated, coupled with the strong mental
attraction set up between persons in earth life
and the spectral form, may cause the latter to
manifest itself to the former, either by more
or less complete materialization, or by partial
manifestation through the physical organism
of the medium, or mediums, present.

In such a case, the spectre, reanimated and
"galvanized" into seeming life by means of
the psychic power of the medium, or those
composing the psychic circle, will strive to
manifest itself by speech, automatic writing,
raps, or otherwise. But, at the best, its efforts
will be feeble and faulty, and the persons witnessing the phenomena will always remember
the same with the dim idea that "there was
something wrong 'about it"—something was
found to be lacking. In some cases, the vibration of old memories will survive in the
spectral form, which will enable it to answer
questions fairly well, and to allude to past
experiences. But even then, in these cases
there will be a shadow of unreality which will
impress the careful observer.

Remember, there are many other forms of "spirit return," partial or complete, but much that passes for the real phenomena is really but a manifestation of the presence of these spectral forms of whose real nature we have been made acquainted by our glimpse into their region of abode. Moreover, these entities (if they may be called by that name) borrow ideas and impressions from the minds of the mediums or persons in the circle, in addition to their own shadowy memories, and thus doubly become reflections or counterfeits.

These spectres have really no soul. The soul which formerly occupied the form has departed to a higher plane, and is in ignorance of the performance of its discarded shell. It is pathetic to witness cases where these counterfeit spectral form are accepted as the departed soul of the individual, by those who loved him in earth life. A lack of knowledge of true occultism often permits of deplorable mistakes of this kind. The true occultist is never deceived in this manner. These spectres are no more "departed souls" or "spirits" than a galvanized physical corpse is the individual which once inhabited it, though the current may cause it to move its muscles and go through the motions of life. It remains a corpse and discarded shell—and. that is just what the spectral form is, plus the remaining vibratory echoes of its old mental life.

CHAPTER VI.

DISEMBODIED SOULS.

YOU very naturally inquire: "But where are the disembodied souls, themselves? I expected to see them as soon as we crossed the border of the Astral!" Yes! that is the general expectation of the neophyte in occultism, when he gets his first glimpse into the Astral scenes. But, unless he happens to stumble at once upon certain sub-planes, he is apt to be disappointed. But, the better way is to let you learn the story by viewing the various sub-planes, at the same time listening to my explanation of that which you witness on them.

You will notice that our vibrations are now changing, and growing more intense. We are now entering upon a very wonderful sub-plane, or rather, upon one of the subdivisions of such a plane. This region, I ask you to remember, is one the entry to which is strictly guarded by the law of the Astral, and watched over by certain very high spiritual influences. It is a sacred place. No one is admitted here as a visitor, unless he be of high spirituality and pure heart. Even a trained occultist, unless he possess these qualifications, finds it impossible to enter these vibrations.

This region is the resting place of the disembodied souls for some time after they have left the physical body. In it they dwell in peaceful slumber, until Nature performs certain work in preparing them for their new plane of life. This stage has been compared to the cocoon-stage, between the stage of the caterpillar and that of the butterfly, in which stage a complete transformation is effected, and the wings of the new life are developed to take the place of the old crawling form.

We are now on this particular sub-plane. Enter upon a contemplation of its wonders, with all reverence and love of all mankind. On all sides, stretching away as far as the eye can see, you perceive the slumbering forms of disembodied souls, each astral form resting in dreamless sleep. And, yet, even if you were not so informed, you would recognize that these forms are not dead, but are merely sleeping. There is none of the atmosphere of death or corpses about this region. Nothing depressing, you notice. Nothing but a sense of infinite calm and peace. Being spiritually developed yourself, you doubtless feel the presence of certain great spiritual entities—though you see them not, because their vibrations are too high for you to see them even by astral vision—these are the great spiritual guardians of this realm, who protect the slumber of the souls at rest herein—the Great Watchers of the Sleeping Souls.

If you will watch carefully, you will notice here and there a movement indicating the awakening of some of these resting forms. A moment later the form disappears from the scene—it seemingly melts into nothingness. But it still is existent—its vibrations simply have changed, and it has moved on to another sub-plane, or division thereof, without having been aware of the scenes of this place. It has begun its real life after death. Let us move on, leaving this scene behind us, while I explain to you some of the phenomena of this period of existence of the disembodied soul. * * * Let us pause here, on the quiet sub-plane, until the matter is made plain to you.

It is a common teaching of many religions that the disembodied soul enters at once upon its heaven or hell. The Roman Catholic Church, and some branches of Buddhism, however, teach of an intermediate state called Purgatory, or a similar name. Some denominations of the Christian Church hold that all souls slumber in unconsciousness, until the call of the great trumpet of Judgment Day, when all awaken from their long sleep and are judged and sent to the place of reward or punishment, as their cases may deserve. You see on the Astral some things which show you that all of these views have a basis in fact, and yet how imperfect are these conceptions of the theologies!

All occultists know, however, that nearly all of the original religious teachers had a very complete knowledge of the real facts of the Astral, and higher planes, and merely handed down to their followers such fragments of the truth as they thought could be assimilated at the time. All of the theological teachings regarding the Life after Death—heavens and hells—contain some truth, but none contain all the truth.

In the majority of cases, the mind of the dying person sinks into the slumber of so-called death, and awakens only after a period of restful, transforming slumber upon the Astral, in the region we have just seen. In some cases, however, there is a brief waking, like a semi-awakening from a dream, shortly after the departure from the physical body, in which case the astral body may appear, visibly, to some friend, associate or loved one—or even in the scenes in which the person usually spent much of his time, as, for instance, his office, shop, study, etc. This accounts for the occasional instances of the disembodied person so appearing, of which there are many well authenticated cases. But even in such event, the disembodied soul soon becomes drowsy, and sinks into the preliminary sleep of the Astral, moving on to the region we have just left.

There is a great difference in the time in which the disembodied soul slumbers in this state. Strange and paradoxical as it may appear, the highest and lowest souls in the scale of development, awaken first. The average soul slumbers far longer than either. I will explain the reason of this to you in a moment.

The highly spiritual person, needing but comparatively little transformation to fit him for the higher planes, may slumber here only a very short time, and then passes on to some of the higher astral planes; or, in cases of high development, may omit these higher astral planes, and pass on at once to the plane or planes above the Astral—into what occultists know as the "heavens," which, technically, are regions of the mental plane, and the ones still higher. The average soul, however, slumbers a much longer time, many years, perhaps, and then awakens upon a higher astral plane suited to its requirements.

The low, material soul, as a rule, awakens very speedily, and passes at once to the low plane for which it has an affinity. But, note this difference: the highly developed soul awakens speedily, for the reason that it has less to slough off and be transformed into higher attributes—the work is already partially performed.

The average soul, on the other hand, requires a much greater transformation for its scenes of higher activities, and so remains much longer in the transforming sleep; and, last (note the seeming paradox, and its explanation), the low, material soul awakens speedily, not because it has been transformed easily for the higher scenes, but, on the contrary, because it is not destined for these higher scenes— it never reaches them, but descends to a low plane of the Astral, where it lives out its low inclinations and ideals, until it finally sickens of them, at least to an extent, and then is ready for further transformation.

All souls, however, high or low, eventually

move off the Astral and enter into the place, or rather the state, of the Mental Plane, or the regions of the "heavens," leaving their astral shells behind them. Some of the highest, as I have said, mount to these planes without any intervening stay on the higher Astral, but the majority have their share of Astral life, higher and lower.

On the "heaven" planes, the spiritual souls spend great periods of time enjoying the well-earned bliss. Souls lower in development spend less time there. The low, material souls, scarcely taste the experience of those high regions. I shall speak further regarding this, as we proceed.

As a general rule, I would remind you, the higher the advancement of a soul, the greater the time between its incarnations; and vice versa. There are special cases, however, such as the call to duty on the part of a high soul, or a strong attraction to another, or others, approaching reincarnation, which may bring back a high soul in a shorter time than it really deserves—this is simply renunciation, however, on the part of the high soul, and is not a violation of the general rule as stated a moment ago.

Let us now change our vibrations, and visit

some of the scenes of Astral life, in which the awakened souls are living, moving, and having their being. A few actual illustrations of life on these planes will teach you more regarding this great subject, than would volumes of books, or years of verbal teaching. Let us begin at some of the lowest sub-planes, and their divisions—the sight is not pleasant, but you will gain a valuable lesson.   *   *   *

CHAPTER VII.

SCENES OF THE ASTRAL.

WE are now vibrating on a very low subdivision of the lowest sub-plane of the Astral. You are conscious of a very unpleasant feeling, and an almost physical repulsion to the atmosphere around you. Some very sensitive natures experience a feeling of being surrounded by a dense, sticky, foul, foggy atmosphere, through which they must almost force their way, when they visit these regions. It is akin to the feelings experienced by a high-minded spiritual person on the earth plane, if he happens to enter a place inhabited by persons of a lewd, vulgar, depraved nature and character—this magnified many degrees by reason of the astral laws.

It is no wonder that one of the old Egyptian writers, whose work survives on graven stone, said, some four thousand years ago: "What manner of foul region is this into which I have foolishly come? It is without water; without air; it is unfathomably deep; it has the darkness of the blackest night, when the sky is overcast with dense clouds, and no ray of

light penetrates their curtain. Souls wander
hopelessly and helplessly about herein; in it
there is no peace, no calm, no rest, no quiet of
the heart or mind. It is an abomination and
desolation. Woe is the soul that abideth
herein!"

Looking around you, in the dim, ghastly
light of this region, you perceive countless
human forms, of the most repulsive appearance. Some of them are so low in the scale
as to seem almost beast-like, rather than
human. There are still lower forms on the
subdivisions just below this one, but I shall
spare you the disgusting sight. These creatures are disembodied souls, in the astral body,
living on the low plane to which they
descended when awakening from their very
brief astral sleep.

If you will peer through the enveloping fog,
you will become conscious of the presence of
the material world as a sort of background.
To you it appears detached, and removed in
space, but to these creatures—these low
souls—the two planes seem to be blended.
To them, they appear actually to be abiding
in the scenes and among the persons of the
lowest phases of earth life. Even you find
that you can see only the very low earth-scenes

in the background—the higher scenes appear blotted out with great smears, like a censored newspaper page in war times. To these poor souls there is no earth world except these scenes which accord with their old desires.

But while apparently living amid these old familiar and congenial low earth-scenes, these souls are really suffering the fate of Tantalus. For while they plainly see these scenes, and all that is going on in them, they cannot otherwise participate in the revels and debaucheries which they perceive plainly—they can SEE only—as for the rest they participate only vicariously. This renders the place a veritable hell for them, for they are constantly tantalized and tormented by sights of scenes in which they cannot participate. They can exercise simply "the lust of the eye," which is but as a thorn in the flesh to them. On all sides, on earth-life, they see their kind (in the flesh) eating, drinking, gambling, engaging in all forms of debauchery and brutality—and while they eagerly cluster around, they cannot make their presence felt (under ordinary circumstances) nor can they participate in the scenes which they witness. The lack of the physical body is indeed a very hell to them, under such circumstances.

The astral atmosphere of low dram-shops, pool rooms, gambling hells, race tracks, "free-and-easies," brothels, "red-light" districts—and their more fashionable counterparts—are filled with these low astral forms of souls across the astral border. Occasionally, they are able to influence some earth companion, who is so saturated with liquor, or overcome by drugs, that he is physically open to such influences. When they so influence him, they strive to lead him into further degradation and debauchery, for, in so doing, they obtain a reflex-gratification, as it were. But I shall not dwell upon this subject—it is too loathsome.

In some instances, the sojourn on this low astral sub-plane sets up such a strong desire for rebirth in the flesh, among similar scenes, that the poor soul eagerly presses forward toward reincarnation on a similar low plane. In other cases, I am glad to say, the experience so sickens and disgusts the poor soul that it experiences a revulsion and disgust for such things, in which case the current of its desires naturally carries it in the opposite direction, and it is given the opportunity to rise in the scale of the Astral, where its better tendencies are encouraged, and a better rebirth finally results.

At the end, however, in nearly all cases

"living-out" results in "out-living," and even
the lowest rises in time. Some few souls,
however, sink so low as to be incapable of rising, and they meet the final fate (not of damna-
tion) of annihilation. Even in these hells of
the astral, however, the degraded souls are
"punished not for their sins, but by them" as
an old writer once forcibly stated it.

But this particular scene is not the only one
on this sub-plane of the Astral—it has many
counterparts. I cannot take time to show them
all to you, or to describe them in detail. I can
illustrate the idea, however, by stating that
close to the scene you have just witnessed, is
another in which the actors are those miserly,
money-loving souls, who have sold all their
better nature for the mess of pottage of
worldly gain. The punishment, by the sin
rather than for it, is similar to that of the low
souls in the preceding scene. They are tormented by the sight, but are tantalized by not
being able to participate. The result is practically similar to that mentioned in the last
case—some find desire increased, and others
find disgust and nausea and thus seek the way
to higher things.

There are hundreds of similar regions on the
lower Astral, some of which are much higher,

however, than those we have just considered.
All of them serve as a Purgatory, or place of
the burning-out of desires of a low kind—not
the burning of material flames, but by the fire
of the desire itself, as we have seen. This idea
of burning away, or purging, of the low
desires, is found to permeate nearly all religions, and has its basis in the facts of the
Astral.

Changing our vibrations, and mounting to
higher sub-planes, we pass rapidly from scene
to scene. You appear astonished to notice
that many of these scenes seem to be set to
scenery, like a great theatre. You notice with
wonder the artificial nature of this astral
scenery, and wonder at the fact that the people
on these scenes seem to regard this scenery
as natural and real, instead of make-believe.
It all seems very shadowy and imperfect to
you, but very real to them. The secret is that
the scenery is the creation of the minds of
those taking part in the scenes, and those who
have preceded them on this plane. It is all
make-believe—a mirage, so to speak—but very
real to those taking part in the scenes.

It is not the purpose of this little book to
describe the chemistry of the Astral by means
of which it is possible for the mind to build

up scenery, etc., from the astral substance. To the advanced occultist, who has studied deeply the occult chemistry, the matter is as simple as is the formation of ice from water, which in turn was once steam—and at the same time as wonderful. The traveller on the Astral always will bear witness to the wonders of that plane, the scenery of which is all built up in this way, though he may not be able to explain the chemistry of its formation.

In this way, on the various higher planes of the Astral, including some of the comparatively lower planes, we find beautiful mountains and valleys, rivers and lakes, cities, towns, villages and country-land—in fact, all forms of scenery known in earth life. We also see buildings of all kinds, and all varieties of household utensils, implements, furniture, etc. All are built from the astral substance by means of the imaginative minds of the dwellers on those planes. To the visitor they seem most unreal—one can actually see through them, and on all sides of them at one time, as in the case of a transparent crystal. But to the dwellers on the Astral they are as solid and real as are their material counterparts— and no doubt regarding their solidity ever enters the mind of the Astral inhabitant.

And what is the purpose of all this theatrical make-believe of the Astral? you well ask. You will see in a moment, when I give you the key that unlocks the secret doors of the Astral life and its meaning.

CHAPTER VIII.

LIFE AND WORK ON THE ASTRAL.

WHAT I have just said regarding the nature of the astral scenery must not be taken as indicating that the Astral, itself, is merely imaginary or unreal in any sense. Nor is the substance of which the scenery is composed any less real than the substance of which the material world is composed. On the material plane, substance manifests as matter; while on the astral plane it manifests in a finer form of "stuff" or material. Again, on the material plane, the material, or matter, is shaped by the physical forces of nature, or, perhaps, by the mind of man using the original material in order to build "artificial" structures or forms.

On the Astral, on the other hand, the astral material is not thrown into shape by physical forces, but is shaped and formed only by the thought and imaginative power of the minds of those inhabiting that plane. But these shapes, forms and structures of the astral material are not to be thought of as existing merely in the mind of the astral dwellers. They have an independent existence of their own, being composed of astral material, though shaped, formed and built up directly by the mind-power of the astral dwellers, instead of by the physical forces of nature.

The astral scenery, etc., survives the passing away of the mind which built it up, and disintegrates only after the passage of considerable time, just as do the material things on the earth plane. As for the power of the imagination of man, do not be deceived for a moment— for this is one of the most efficient powers in nature, and operates strongly even on the material plane, though on the Astral its power is more easily recognized by the senses. To the dwellers on the Astral, their scenery, buildings, etc., are as solid as are those of the material plane to the dwellers thereupon.

Passing through the various sub-planes, and their divisions, on the Astral you notice a great variety of scenery, and a great difference in the character and occupations of the inhabitants. But, you notice one general characteristic underlying all of the differences, namely, the fact that all of these persons (astral dwellers) seem to be filled with an intense earnestness, and manifest a degree of concentration which gives to them an appearance of being preoccupied. This, often, to such an extent that they seem to be oblivious to our presence and passage through their midst, unless we address them directly. Again, everyone seems to be busy, even when their tasks are those of sport or play.

The key to the occupation and pursuits of the dwellers on the Astral is found in the principle that the life of the soul on the comparatively higher divisions of the Astral consists in a working out of the intellectual desires, and ordinary tendencies, tastes, likes, and aspirations which they were unable to manifest fully in earth life. I do not mean the low sensual desires, or purely animal tastes, but rather the "ambitions" and similar forms of desire or strong inclinations. Many of these inclinations may be very creditable and praiseworthy, rather than otherwise, but they are all concerned with physical manifestations, rather than with spiritual unfoldment and evolution in the strict sense of these terms. The higher planes are those in which the spiritual forces bud and flower, and bear fruit—the Astral, even on its highest planes, is the scene of the living-out, and working-out, of earthly intellectual and similar ambitions and aspirations.

The higher the plane of the Astral world, the less are the old earth scenes in evidence, even in the shape of the dim background we saw as we progressed on our journey. As we mounted on the scale, these old earth scenes grew very dim, and where we are standing now, on the fourth sub-plane, they are practically out of sight. This particular sub-plane is not particularly elevating, but nevertheless is interesting to the student.

As we pass from scene to scene, we see the "happy hunting grounds" of the American Indians, thickly settled with these old aborigines who have been dwelling there for quite a period of time. They are busy, and happy hunting their astral buffaloes, and other game (all artificially created by their imagination, from the astral substance, and having no real existence as living, feeling animals). A little further on, we witness similar forms of the "Spirit-land" of other primitive people, in some of which the disembodied warriors fight and conquer great hosts of artificial foes, and then have great feasts according to their old customs.

Valhalla is here, as well as the other imaginary Paradises of the old races of men. But their inhabitants are dwindling in number, being caught up in the current bearing them on to reincarnation. But, note this, that while there is nothing elevating in the pursuits followed in these scenes, there is nothing degrading or lowering, from a strictly spiritual point of view. But, there is in evidence always a living-out, and wearing-out, of the old desires of this kind, to make room for higher ones—all tends toward spiritual evolution.

Raising our vibrations rapidly, and passing over many degrees of scenes of this kind, we find ourselves on a considerably higher plane. Here we see men engaged in what would be called "useful work" in earth life. But they are performing it not as labor, but rather as a joyous recreation. Observing closely, you will see that the work is all of an inventive and constructive nature. The men and women are perfecting that in which their interest was engaged while on earth life. They are improving on their work, and are filled with the joy of creation. They remind one forcibly of Kipling's mention of the future state when: " . . . no one shall work for money, and no one shall work for fame; but each for the joy of the working." On some of these subdivisions we see the artist busily at work, turning out wonderful masterpieces; also musicians creating great compositions, of which they had vainly dreamt while in earth-

life.   The architect builds great structures—
the inventor discovers great things.   And all
are filled with the joy of work, and the ecstacy
of creative imagination.

But, make not the mistake, student, of regarding this as merely play, or as possibly a
form of reward for well-done world work,
though, of course, both of these elements play
their part in the general working of the Law.
The main thing to remember is that in this
work on the Astral, there is an actual mental
advance and progress.

Moreover, in many cases, here on these very
planes of the Astral there is being built the
mould from which will actually pour great inventive and creative achievements, on the material plane, in the future incarnations of these
souls now doing work on this plane.   The Astral is the great pattern shop of the world.
Its patterns are reproduced in matter when the
soul revisits the earth scenes.   Many a work
of art, musical composition, great piece of lit-
erature, or great invention, has been but a re-
production of an Astral pattern.   This will
help to explain the feeling common to all great
performers of creative, imaginative or intellectual work—the strange feeling that their
work is but a completion of something at which

they had previously wrought—a re-discovery,
as it were.

Again, in this work-play of the Astral, the
soul is always at work using up old ideas,
aspirations, etc., and discarding them finally.
In this way real progress is made, for after all
even earth-life is seen to be largely a matter of
"living-out and out-living"—of mounting
higher on the steps of each mistake and each
failure. In the work of the Astral many old
ideas are worked out and discarded; many
old longings exhausted and discarded; many
old ambitions manifested and then left behind
on the trail. There is a certain "burning up,
and burning out" of old mental material, and a
place made for new and better material in the
new earth life. Often, in this way, on the Astral there is accomplished as much in the direction of improvement and progress, as would be
possible only in quite a number of earth-
lives. Life on the Astral is very earnest and
intense—the vibrations are much higher than
on the material plane.

Bearing this principle in mind, these Astral
scenes which you are now witnessing take on
a great and new meaning. You recognize them
as very important school-rooms in the great
school of life. Work is being done here that

can not be accomplished elsewhere. Everything has its meaning. There is no waste effort, or useless activity in the universe, no matter what the careless observer may say to the contrary. The Astral is no joke of the universe—it is one of its great, real workshops and laboratories of the soul. It has its distinct place in the work of spiritual unfoldment and evolution.

CHAPTER IX.

HIGHER PLANES AND BEYOND.

RAISING our vibrations a little, we now enter upon the great second sub-plane of the Astral, with its seven subdivisions and its many minor divisions and regions. Almost before I tell you, you will feel the religious atmosphere pervading this region. For this is the plane upon which the religious aspirations and emotions find full power of expression. On this sub-plane are many souls who have spent some time on the other sub-planes of the Astral, doing their work there and then passing on to these scenes in order, to manifest this part of their natures.

But, I wish to call your attention to the occult distinction between "spirituality" and "religion." Spirituality is the recognition of the divine spark within the soul, and the unfoldment of the same into consciousness; while religion, in the occult sense, consists of observance of certain forms of worship, rites, ceremonies, etc., the holding to certain forms of theology, and the manifestation of what may be called the religious emotions. The religious instinct is deeply implanted in the hearts of

men, and may be called the stepping-stone toward true spirituality—but it is not spirituality
itself. In its higher forms, it is a beautiful
thing, but in its lower ones it leads to narrow-
ness and bigotry—but it is a necessary step on
the Path, and all must mount it in order to
reach higher things.

This second sub-plane of the Astral is filled
with a multitude of souls each of whom is en-
deavoring to manifest and express his own
particular shade of religious conception. It
may be said to contain all the heavens that
have ever been dreamed of in theology, and
taught in the churches—each filled with devotees of the various creeds. Each of the great
religions has its own particular region, in which
its disciples gather, worship, and rejoice. In
each region the religious soul finds "just what
he had expected" and hoped to find on "the
other shore." Some remain content in their
own place, while others growing dissatisfied
drift toward some sub-region, or group, which
comes nearer to their newly awakened conception of truth.

In passing rapidly through these regions,
you will find that each has its own particular
environment in exact accordance with the beliefs of the persons inhabiting it. Some have

the appearance of a plain, old-fashioned meeting house, on an immense scale; while others resemble a gigantic cathedral, filled with gorgeous decorations and paraphernalia, and echoing with the sound of glorious litanies and other ritualistic forms of worship. Each has its officiating priests or preachers, according to its regulations. You see at a glance that the environment, scenery, buildings, decorations, etc., are built up from the astral substance by the imaginative power of the minds of those congregating at each point. All the stage-setting and properties are found fully in evidence (I say this in all seriousness, and with no attempt to be frivolous or flippant)—you may even see the golden crowns, harps, and stiff haloes, in some cases, and hear the sound of "the eternal chant of praise."

I regret to be compelled to call your attention to the regions of some lower forms of religion, in which there is a background picture of a burning hell, at which the devotees gaze with satisfaction, feeling the joy of heaven intensified by the sight of the suffering souls in hell. It is a satisfaction to tell you that the suffering souls, and their hell, are but fictitious things created by the imagination from the astral substance—a mere stage setting as it were. Dante's Inferno has its adequate counterparts on the Astral Plane.

I ask you, particularly to gaze upon this most horrible scene before us. A large severely furnished edifice is shown, with seated congregation wearing stern, hard, cruel faces. They gaze toward the top of a smoking bottomless pit, from which rises a sort of great, endless chain, each link having a huge sharp hook upon which is impaled a doomed soul. This soul is supposed to rise to the top of the pit once in a thousand years, and as each appears it is heard to cry in mournful accents: "How long—how long?" To this agonized question, a deep stern voice is heard replying: "Forever! Forever!" I am glad to tell you that this congregation is dwindling, many evolving to higher conceptions, and practically no new recruits arriving from the earth-plane to fill the depleting ranks. In time, this congregation will disappear entirely, and the ghastly stage scenery and properties will gradually dissolve into astral dust and fade from sight forever.

All forms of religion, high and low, oriental and occidental, ancient and modern, are represented on this plane. Each has its own particular abode. It would delight the heart of a student of comparative religion to visit these scenes. There are some beautiful and inspiring scenes and regions on this plane, filled with advanced souls and beautiful characters. But, alas! there are some repulsive ones also. It is marvellous, in viewing these scenes, to realize how many forms human religion and theology has taken in its evolution. Every form of deity has its region, with its worshippers. It is interesting to visit the scenes once filled with the worshippers of the most ancient religions. Many have only a handful of worshippers remaining on this plane; while in some cases, the worshippers have entirely disappeared, and the astral scenery of the region, its temples and shrines, are crumbling away and disappearing just as have the old temples disappeared on the material plane.

On the highest of the sub-planes of the Astral we find many regions inhabited by the philosophers, scientists, metaphysicians, and higher theologians of the race—those who used their intellectual power in striving to solve the Riddle of the Universe, and to peer Behind the Veil, by the use of intellect alone. High and low are met with here. There are as many schools of philosophy and metaphysics here, as there were religious sects on the plane below.

Some are pitifully weak, crude and childish in their conceptions—others have advanced so far that they seem like demi-gods of intellect. But even this is not true "spirituality," any more than is the religious formalism and dogmas of the plane below. All has its place, however, and everything is evolving and unfolding.

It is interesting to note then on this plane, and the one below, are to be found groups of disembodied souls who persist in declaring that "there is no hereafter for the soul;" "the soul perishes with the body;" etc. These deluded souls believe that they are still on the material plane, in spite of appearances, and they have built up quite a good counterfeit earth-scenery to sustain them. They sneer and sniff at all talk of life outside of the physical body, and bang their astral tables with their astral fists, to prove how solid all real things are—they believe only that which is solid and "real." This, indeed, is the very irony of astral life.

You have noticed certain glorious forms on these regions, student, as we have passed through these scenes, and I have promised to inform you as to their character. These were those highly evolved beings, once men like ourselves, who have voluntarily returned from higher spheres to teach and instruct along the lines of religion and philosophy, combining the best of both, and leading upward toward Truth those souls who have arrived at a possible understanding of these things. It is verily true, on the Astral as well as on the earth plane, that "when the pupil is ready, the Master appears." The Astral has many, very many of these Elder Brothers of the Race, working diligently and earnestly for the uplift of those struggling on the Path.

I may say here, that an understanding of the nature of the various regions of the Astral, and the scenes thereof, will throw light upon the fact that the reports of "the other side" given by disembodied souls at spiritualistic seances, etc., are so full of contradictions and discrepancies, no two seeming to agree. The secret is that each is telling the truth as he sees it in the Astral, without realizing the nature of what they have seen, or the fact that it is, at the best, merely one aspect among millions of others. Contrast the varying "heavens" just mentioned, and see how different the reports would be coming from some of their inhabitants. When the nature of astral phenomena is once understood, the difficulty vanishes, and each report is recognized as being an attempt to describe the Astral picture upon which the disembodied entity has gazed, believing it to be actual and real.

I wish here to tell you, student, some little about the planes higher than the Astral. These planes transcend adequate description. Enough to say, here, that each soul on the Astral, even the very lowest, finally sinks into an astral slumber when it has completed its work on that plane. Before passing on to rebirth, however, it awakens for a time upon one of the subdivisions of the next highest plane above the Astral. It may remain awake on this plane, in its appropriate subdivision, for merely a moment of time, or for many centuries even, depending upon its state of spiritual unfoldment. During this stay on these higher planes, the soul communes with the higher phase of itself—the divine fragment of Spirit—and is strengthened and invigorated thereby. In this period of communion, much dross of the nature is burnt out and dissolved into nothingness, and the higher part of the nature is nourished and encouraged.

These higher planes of Being constitute the real "heaven world" of the soul. The more highly advanced the soul, the longer does it

abide between incarnations on these planes.
Just as the mind is developed and enabled to
express its longings and ambitions, on the Astral, so is the higher portions of the soul
strengthened and developed on these higher
planes.   The joy, happiness and spiritual
blessedness of these higher planes are beyond
ordinary words. So wonderful are they, that
even long after the soul has been born again
on earth, there will arise within it memories
of its experiences upon those higher planes,
and it will sigh for a return to them, as a dove
sighs for its far-off home towards which its
weary wings urge its flight. Once heard, the
harmony of the heaven-world is never forgot-
ten—its memories remain to strengthen us in
moments of trial and sorrow.

These, then, are the real "heaven worlds"
of the occult teachings—something far different from even the highest Astral planes.
The reports of the mystics are based on experiences on these planes, not upon those of
the Astral. Your soul has truly informed you
regarding the reality of the existence of these
wonderful regions and scenes—it has not deceived you. Therefore, hold fast to the ideal
and the vision—follow the gleam, follow the
gleam!

CHAPTER X.

THE ASTRAL LIGHT.

IT must not be supposed for a moment that the Astral is simply a plane of Nature created for a place of temporary abode and development for souls which have passed out of the physical body—a mere stopping place between reincarnations. Important as are the planes of the Astral in the progress of the disembodied souls, they form but one phase of the activities of this great plane of Nature. Indeed, even eliminating the disembodied souls from the Astral, there would be enough strange and wonderful phenomena on that plane, as well as enough wonderful inhabitants and dwellers on some of its subplanes, to still render it the place and region of interest that it always has been to occultists. Before we finish our astral journey, and return to earth life, let us take a hasty glance at these wonderful phases of astral phenomena and life.

THE ASTRAL LIGHT. Changing our vibrations, we find ourselves entering a strange region, the nature of which at first you fail to discern. Pausing a moment until your astral vision becomes attuned to the peculiar vibrations of this region, you find that you are becoming gradually aware of what may be called an immense picture gallery, spreading out in all directions, and apparently bearing a direct relation to every point of space on the surface of the earth.

At first you find it difficult to decipher the meaning of this great array of pictures. The trouble arises from the fact that they are arranged not one after the other in sequence on a flat plane, but rather in sequence, one after another in a peculiar order which may be called the order of "X-ness in space," because it is neither the dimension of length, breadth, or depth—it is practically the order of the fourth dimension of space, which cannot be described in terms of ordinary spatial dimension.

Again, you find, upon closely examining the pictures that they are very minute—practically microscopic in size—and require the use of the peculiar magnifying power of astral vision to bring them up to a size capable of being recognized by your faculty of visual recognition.

The astral vision, when developed, is capable of magnifying any object, material or astral, to an enormous degree—for instance, the trained occultist is able to perceive the whirling atoms and corpuscles of matter, by means of this peculiarity of astral vision. Likewise, he is able to plainly perceive many fine vibrations of light which are invisible to the ordinary sight. In fact, the peculiar Astral Light which pervades this region is due to the power of the astral vision to receive and register these fine vibrations of light.

Bring this power of magnifying into operation, you will see that each of the little points and details of the great world picture so spread before you in the Astral Light, is really a complete scene of a certain place on earth, at a certain period in the history of the earth. It resembles one of the small views in a series of moving pictures—a single view on the roll of film. It is fixed and not in motion, and yet we can move forward along the fourth dimension, and thus obtain a moving picture of the history of any point on the surface of the earth, or even combine the various points into a larger moving picture, in the same way. Let us prove this by actual experiment.

Close your eyes for a moment, while we travel back in time (so to speak) along the series of these astral records—for, indeed, they travel back to the beginning of the history of the earth. Now open your eyes! Looking around you, you perceive the pictured representation of strange scenes filled with persons wearing a peculiar garb—but all is still, no life, no motion.

Now, let us move forward in time, at a much higher rate than that in which the astral views were registered. You now see flying before you the great movement of life on a certain point of space, in a far distant age. From birth to death you see the life of these strange people, all in the space of a few moments. Great battles are fought, and cities rise before your eyes, all in a great moving picture flying at a tremendous speed.

Now stop, and then let us move backward in time, still gazing at the moving pictures. You see a strange sight, like that of "reversing the film" in a moving picture. You see everything moving backward—cities crumbling into nothingness, men rising from their graves, and growing younger each second until they are finally born as babes—everything moving backward in time, instead of forward.

You can thus witness any great historical event, or follow the career of any great personage from birth to death—or backward. You will notice, moreover, that everything is semi-transparent, and that accordingly, you can see the picture of what is going on inside of buildings as well as outside of them. Nothing escapes the Astral Light Records. Nothing can be concealed from it.

You have gazed at the great World Picture in the Records of the Astral Light—the great Akashic Records, as we Hindus call it. In these records are to be found pictures of every single event, without exception, that has ever happened in the history of the earth—recorded just exactly as it really happened, moreover, the record being ultra-photographic and including the smallest detail.

By travelling to a point in time, on the fourth dimension, you may begin at that point, and see a moving picture of the history of any part of the earth from that time on to the present— or you may reverse the sequence by travelling backward, as we have seen. You may also travel in the Astral, on ordinary space dimensions, and thus see what happened simultaneously all over the earth, at any special moment of time, if you wish.

As a matter of strict truth, however, I must inform you that the real records of the past— the great Akashic Records—really exist on a much higher plane than the Astral, and that which you have witnessed is but a reflection (practically perfect, however) of the original records.

It requires a high degree of occult development in order to perceive even this reflection in the Astral Light, and unaided by my own power you could not perceive these sights at this time. An ordinary clairvoyant, however, is often able to catch occasional glimpses of these astral pictures, and may thus describe fairly well the happenings of the past. In the same way, the psychometrist, given an object, may be able to give the past history of the object, including a description of the persons associated therewith.

CHAPTER XI.

ASTRAL ENTITIES.

WITHOUT intending to go deeply into this subject—for the same is reserved for the sole teaching of the advanced pupil, and must not be carelessly spread before others—I think it well to call your attention to the fact that on certain planes of the Astral, there exist certain entities, or living beings, which never were human, and never will be, for they belong to an entirely different order of nature.

These strange entities are ordinarily invisible to human beings, but under certain conditions they may be sensed by the astral vision. Strictly speaking, these strange beings do not dwell upon the Astral at all—that is, not in the sense of the Astral as a part of space, or a place. We call them Astral entities simply because they become visible for the first time to man, when he is able to vision on the Astral, or by means of the astral senses—and for no other reason.

So far as place, or space, is concerned these entities or being dwell upon the earth, just as do the human beings. They vibrate differently from us, that is all. They are also usually of but a microscopic size, and would be invisible to the human eye even if they vibrated on the same plane as do we. The astral vision not only senses their vibrations, under certain conditions, but also, under certain other conditions, it magnifies their forms into perceptible size.

Some of these astral entities are known as Nature Spirits, and inhabit streams, rocks, mountains, forests, etc. Their occasional appearance to persons of psychic temperament, or in whom a degree of astral vision has been awakened, has given rise to the numerous tales and legends in the folk-lore of all nations regarding a strange order of beings, to which various names have been given, as for instance: fairies, pixies, elves, brownies, peris, djinns, trolls, satyrs, fauns, kobolds, imps, goblins, little folk, tiny people, etc., etc., and similar names found in the mythologies and legends of all people. The old occultists called the earth entities of this class by the name of "gnomes;" the air entities as "sylphs;" the water beings as "undines;" and the fire, or ether, beings as "salamanders."

This class of astral entities, as a rule, avoid the presence of man, and fly from places in which he dwells—for instance they avoid large cities as men avoid a cemetery. They prefer the solitudes of nature, and resent the onward march of men which drives them further and further into new regions. They do not object to the physical presence of man, so much as they do his mental vibrations which are plainly felt by them, and which are very distasteful to them.

A certain class of them are what may be called "good fellows," and these, once in a while, seem to find pleasure in helping and aiding human beings to whom they have formed an attachment. Many such cases are related in the folk lore of the older countries, but modern life has driven these friendly helpers from the scene, in most places.

Another class, now also very uncommon, seems to find delight in playing elfish, childish pranks, particularly in the nature of practical jokes upon peasants, etc. At spiritualistic seances, and similar places, these elfish pranks are sometimes in evidence.

The ancient magicians and wonder workers were often assisted by creatures of this class. And, even today in India, Persia, China, and other Oriental lands, such assistance is not unknown; and many of the wonderful feats of these magicians are attributable only to such aid.

As a rule, as J have said, these creatures are not unfriendly to man, though they may play a prank with him occasionally, under some' circumstances. They seem particularly apt to play tricks upon neophytes in psychic research, who seek to penetrate the Astral without proper instruction, and without taking the proper precautions. To such a one they may appear as hideous forms, monsters, etc., and thus drive him away from the plane in which their presence may become apparent to him.

However, they usually pay no attention to the advanced occultist, and either severely let him alone, or else flee his presence—though cases are not unknown, in the experience of the majority of advanced occultists, when some of these little folk seem anxious and willing to be of aid to the earnest, conscientious inquirer, who recognizes them as a part of nature's great manifestation, and not as an "unnatural" creature, or vile monstrosity.

ARTIFICIAL ENTITIES. In addition to the non-human entities which are perceived by astral vision, or on the Astral plane—including a number of varietites and classes other than those mentioned by me, and to which I purposely have omitted reference for reasons which will be recognized as valid by all true occultists—there are to be found on the Astral, or on the earth plane by means of astral vision, a great class of entities, or semi-entities, which occultists know as "artificial entities."

These artificial entities were not born in the natural manner, nor created by the ordinary creative forces of nature. They are the creations of the minds of men, and are really a highly concentrated class of thought-forms. They are not entities, in the strict sense of the term, having no life or vitality except that which they borrow from, or have been given by their creators. The student of occultism who has grasped the principle of the creation of thought-forms, will readily grasp the nature, power, and limitations of this class of dwellers in the Astral.

The majority of these artificial entities, or thought-forms, are created unconsciously by persons who manifest strong desire-force, accompanied by definite mental pictures of that which they desire. But many have learned the art of creating them consciously, in an elementary form of magic, white or black. Much of the effect of thought-force, or mind-power, is due to the creation of these thought-forms.

Strong wishes for good, as well as strong curses for evil, tend to manifest form and a semblance of vitality in the shape of these artificial entities. These entities, however, are under the law of thought-attraction, and go only where they are attracted. Moreover, they may be neutralized, and even destroyed, by positive thought properly directed in the way known to all advanced students along these lines.

Another, and quite a large, class of these artificial Astral entities, consist of thought-forms of supernatural (!) beings, sent out by the strong mental pictures, oft repeated, of the persons creating them—the creator usually being unconscious of the result. For instance, a strongly religious mother, who prays for the protective influence of the angels around and about her children, and whose strong religious imagination pictures these heavenly visitors as present by the side of the children, frequently actually creates thought-forms of such angel guardians around her children, who are given a degree of life and mind vibrations from the soul of the mother. In this way, such guardian angels, so created, serve to protect the children and warn them from evil and against temptation. Many a pious mother has accomplished more than she realized by her prayers and earnest desires. The early fathers of the churches, occidental and oriental, were aware of this fact, and consequently bade their followers to use this form of prayer and thought, though they did not explain the true underlying reason. Even after the mother has passed on to higher planes, her loving memory may serve to keep alive these thought-form entities, and thus serve to guard her loved ones.

In a similar way, many "family ghosts" have been created and kept in being in the same way, by the constantly repeated tale and belief in their reality, on the part of generation after generation. In this class belong the celebrated historic ghosts who warn royal or noble families of approaching death or sorrow. The familiar family ghosts walking the walls of old castles on certain anniversaries, are usually found to belong to this class (though not always so).

Many haunted houses are explained in this way, also—the ghost may be "laid" by anyone familiar with the laws of thought-forms. It must be remembered that these artificial entities are of purely human creation, and obtain all their apparent and mind from the action of the thought-force of their creators. Repeated thought, and repeated belief, will serve to keep alive and to strengthen these entities—otherwise they will disappear in time.

Many supernatural visitors, saints, semi-divine beings, etc., of all religions have been formed in this way, and, in many cases, are kept in being by the faith of the devotees of the church, chapel, or shrine. In many temples in oriental countries, there have been created, and kept alive for many centuries, the thought-form entities of the minor gods and saints, endowed in thought with great power of response to prayer, offering, and ceremonies. Those accepting the belief in these powers, are brought into harmony with its vibrations, and are effected thereby, for good or evil.

The power of the devils of savage races (some of whom practically are devil-worshippers), arise in the same way. Even in the early history of the western religions, we find many references to the appearance of the Devil, and of his evil work; witchcraft diabolical presences, etc., all of which were created thought-form entities of this kind. Many of the effects of sorcery, black-magic, etc., were produced in this way—the element of belief, of course, adding greatly to the effect. The Voodoo practices of Africa, and later, of Martinique; and the Kahuna practices of Hawaii, are based on these same principles. The effect of "charms," etc., depend on the same laws, including the effect of faith.

Even certain forms of "spirits," so-called, of certain forms of spiritualistic seances arise from this principle, and have never been human beings, at all. An understanding of this principle will aid in the interpretation of many puzzling phases of psychic phenomena.

"SPIRIT RETURN." Nothing that I have said must be taken as denying the reality and validity of what the western world knows as "spirit return." On the other hand, I am fully familiar with very many instances of the real return to earth-life of disembodied souls. But at the same time, I, as well as all other advanced occultists, are equally aware of the many chances of mistake in this class of psychic phenomena. Shades, and even astral shells, too often are mistaken for departed loved ones. Again, many apparently real "spirit forms" are nothing more or less than semi-vitalized thought-form artificial entities such as I have just described.

Again, many mediums are really clairvoyant, and are able to unconsciously draw to some extent upon the Astral Records for their information regarding the past, instead of receiving the communication from a disembodied soul—in all honesty and in good faith, in many cases. Occultism does not deny the phenomena of modern western spiritualism—it merely seeks to explain its true nature, and to verify some of it while pointing out the real nature of others. It should be welcomed as an ally, by all true spiritualists.

ASTRAL VISION. . It must not be supposed that the astral vision dawns suddenly upon anyone, in full force. Rather is it a matter of slow gradual development in the majority of cases. Many persons possess it to a faint degree, and fail to develop it further, for want of proper instruction. Many persons have occasional flashes of it, and are entirely without it at other times. Many "feel" the astral vibrations, rather than seeing with the astral vision. Others, gain a degree of astral vision by means of crystal gazing, etc. That which is frequently referred to as "psychic sight," or "psychic sensing," is a form of astral visioning or sensing. Psychism is bound up with astral phenomena, in all cases.

* * * * * * * *

In this little manual, I have sought to give

you, in a few lines, the great underlying facts of the Astral Plane. I have crowded very much into a very small space, so that you will have to read and study my words very carefully, in order to get the full meaning. In fact, this is not a book to be read on and then laid aside—rather, it should be re-read and re-studied, until all the essence is extracted.

* * * * * * * *

The glimpses of a number of the sub-planes of the Astral should give you a general, clear idea of many other scenes on that great plane. Remember, these scenes are typical of those witnessed by any advanced occultist who is able to travel on those planes—as you, yourself, may verify when you are able to vision on these planes. They are under-drawn, rather than overdrawn. Some of the more startling and "sensational" scenes have been omitted altogether, as I have no desire to attract, or cater to, those seeking sensation—my work is for the earnest student, alone.

* * * * * * * *

Use this manual as a key to unlock many mysteries—not as a book to while away an idle hour. Do not have any "idle hours." Do not try to "kill time." Be an earnest, thoughtful, occultist, ever unfolding and evolving as you progress along The Path! Look Forward, not Backward! Look Upward, not Downward! Have Faith, not Fear! For, within your soul is a Spark of the Divine Flame, which cannot be extinguished!

Triumph of the Human Spirit: The Greatest Achievements of the Human Soul and How Its Power Can Change Your Life, by Paul Tice. A triumph of the human spirit happens when we know we are right about something, put our heart into achieving its goal, and then succeed. There is no better feeling. People throughout history have triumphed while fighting for the highest ideal of all -- spiritual truth. Tice brings you back to relive and explore history's most incredible spiritual moments, bringing you into the lives of visionaries and great leaders who were in touch with their souls and followed their hearts. They explored God in their own way, exposed corruption and false teachings, or freed themselves and others from suppression. People like Gandhi, Joan of Arc, and Dr. King expressed exactly what they believed and changed the entire course of history. They were eliminated through violence, but on a spiritual level achieved victory because of their strong moral cause. Their spirit lives on, and the world was greatly improved. Tice covers other movements and people who may have physically failed, but spiritually triumphed. This book not only documents the history of spiritual giants, it shows how you can achieve your own spiritual triumph. In today's world we are free to explore the truth without fear of being tortured or executed. As a result, the rewards are great. Various exercises will strengthen the soul and reveal its hidden power. One can discover their true spiritual source with this work and will be able to tap into it. This is the perfect book for all those who believe in spiritual freedom and have a passion for the truth. **ISBN 1-885395-57-4 · 295 pages · 6 x 9 · trade paper · illustrated · $19.95**

Mysteries Explored: The Search for Human Origins, UFOs, and Religious Beginnings, by Jack Barranger and Paul Tice. Jack Barranger and Paul Tice are two authors who have combined forces in an overall investigation into human origins, religion, mythology, UFOs, and other unexplained phenomena. In the first chapter, "The Legacy of Zecharia Sitchin", Barranger covers the importance of Sitchin's *Earth Chronicles* books, which is creating a revolution in the way we look at our past. In "The First Dragon" chapter, Tice examines the earliest known story containing dragons, coming from Sumerian/Babylonian mythology. In "Past Shock", Barranger suggests that events which happened thousands of years ago very strongly impact humanity today. In "UFOs: From Earth or Outer Space?" Tice explores the evidence for aliens being from other earthly dimensions as opposed to having an extraterrestrial origin. "Is Religion Harmful?" looks at the origins of religion and why the entire idea may no longer be working for us, while "A Call to Heresy" shows how Jesus and the Buddha were considered heretics in their day, and how we have reached a critical point in our present spiritual development that requires another such leap. Aside from these chapters, the book also contains a number of outrageous (but discontinued) newsletters, including: Promethean Fire, Pleiadian Poop, and Intrusions. **ISBN 1-58509-101-4 · 104 pages · 6 x 9 · trade paper · $12.95**

Mushrooms and Mankind: The Impact of Mushrooms on Human Consciousness and Religion, by James Arthur. For thousands of years on our planet, humanity has been involved in a symbiotic relationship with plants. Not only have plants supplied mankind with a never-ending food source, the necessary nourishment for our bodies and life itself, but they have also served us in another way: an extremely important and intricate one, yet an often overlooked one. This book uncovers the natural link between man, consciousness, and God. This discovery may at first seem abstract, wishful thinking, or even impossible; yet as evidence presented on these pages unfolds, you may find that its understanding does not require as much of a leap of faith as you might think. This may be the most significant discovery in the entire field of religious knowledge ever to happen in the history of mankind. Should people use

this knowledge, it will allow many on this planet to put their differences aside, and join in the understanding that each and every one of us may now experience that which has been, until this time, hidden away in the recesses of our spiritual history. We may at last be able to open ourselves to an entirely new and valuable consciousness. **ISBN 1-58509-151-0 · 180 pages · 6 x 9 · trade paper · $16.95**

Vril or Vital Magnetism, **with an introduction by Paul Tice.** Vril is another name for the life energy of the body, known in other cultures worldwide as mana, prana, chi, or vital force. Most of the ancient cultures of the world were aware of this important force and worked to make use of it. In today's world, especially in the West, we move along through life completely oblivious to this truly vital energy. Although this force cannot be seen, it is the life force within our bodies. It takes energy from food and provides muscles with energy, which in turn allows us to move about in daily life as well as grow and metabolize. Nourishment, digestion, and elimination are all driven by the life force. Vril also has a connection to the mind, and methods can be employed to store up its energy and use it constructively. Vril is not manufactured in the human body, but can be collected and used effectively. This energy 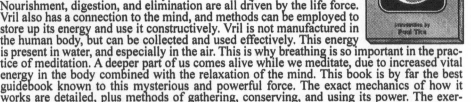 is present in water, and especially in the air. This is why breathing is so important in the practice of meditation. A deeper part of us comes alive while we meditate, due to increased vital energy in the body combined with the relaxation of the mind. This book is by far the best guidebook known to this mysterious and powerful force. The exact mechanics of how it works are detailed, plus methods of gathering, conserving, and using its power. The exercises given are powerful and they work. This is really more of a self-help book than a simple fact book or mystical overview. **ISBN 1-58509-030-1 • 124 pages • 5 1/2 x 8 1/2 • trade paper • $12.95**

The Odic Force: Letters on Od and Magnetism, **by Karl von Reichenbach.** What is the Odic force? This is a vital energy or life force that permeates all living plants, animals, and humans. Von Reichenbach was the first person to approach this force scientifically, having conducted hundreds of careful experiments. He began to work with people who were sensitive enough to accurately detect the polarity of magnets because they could *see* it. These people could also see the human aura—an energy field connected to the human body, plus detect an energy-related color spectrum that was directly linked to metals and minerals. Many of these findings were later backed up by a brilliant man in the twentieth century named Wilhelm Reich. Von Reichenbach wrote this book as a simplified version of a more advanced text, making the work easy to study for those who wish to grasp the subject. With this book, there is no better place to start. It is our hope that such material, and a more complete understanding of it, can move humanity's understanding of itself and the universe forward. **ISBN 1-58509-001-8 • 192 pages • 6 x 9 • trade paper • $15.95**

The New Revelation: The Coming of a New Spiritual Paradigm, **by Arthur Conan Doyle.** Arthur Conan Doyle was a famous mystery writer (*The Adventures of Sherlock Holmes*) and spiritualist from the early twentieth century who predicted, with this book, the coming of a spiritually based religion in the future. This "New Revelation" seems to have taken shape. as he had predicted, in the form of the New Age Movement. Doyle based this book on the spiritualist movement of his day which included channeling, seances, automatic writing, and a variety of other strange, psychic occurrences. He investigated these things thoroughly and came away convinced that more proof existed within these realms than could be found within any standard religion. He acknowledged some of the fraudulent scams that were exposed in spiritual circles and stated that serious researchers  like himself completely deplored such events and that they were not representative of the larger areas of authentic psychic phenomena. As our more modern research continues, we may be able to clear up some of the deeper mysteries concerning who we are and where we go after death. If this should happen it would truly qualify as a "new revelation", one that would shake our religious foundations to the core. The "Old Revelation", Doyle says, has lost its power through bigotry, mismanagement, materialism, and claims of infallibility that no longer hold up. A new world of personal discovery awaits us, as an alternative, and one can begin to explore it now by reading this classic work. **ISBN 1-58509-220-7 • 124 pages • 6 x 9 • trade paper • $12.95**

***Reason and Belief: The Impact of Scientific Discovery on Religious and Spiritual Faith*, by Sir Oliver Lodge.** Sir Oliver Lodge was a respected writer from the early twentieth century. At this time, there were a number of scientific advances that caused one to consider the ramifications of these new discoveries on the religious and spiritual beliefs of the day. But the impact of science may not be so great on spiritual matters in the final analysis, according to Lodge. He puts forth a number of interesting examples. He does not champion science as the final answer, which is what makes this book so interesting. Science is still helpful. It is a tool that is allowing us to reach spiritual answers that have so far not been found. Lodge actively searches for spiritual answers with great wisdom throughout the book and, when necessary, backs off from his great spiritual knowledge and explores our grasp of science to help us along. The last third of the book covers the scope of science. Lodge is a mystic who states that science is useful, but will never embrace the whole of knowledge. Thinking that science is and will be the final answer is the mistake in thinking that scientists of today fall into. They often ignore the seers and prophets of the past who have given us great spiritual truths. Scientists depend solely on a limited bandwidth of discipline that sometimes creates blinders, as found on a racehorse that can only run in a straight line. If the answer is off to the side, as part of the infinite world around us, it will never be seen. Lodge takes the blinders off, and opens us up to the larger possibilities around us. **ISBN 1-58509-226-6 • 180 pages • 6 x 9 • trade paper • $17.95**

***William Blake: A Biography*, by Basil De Selincourt.** William Blake was a great painter, poet, and mystic who rejected science and reason and preferred using the powers of imagination in his quest for truth. Because of his psychological and visionary views, he was considered a forerunner to Freud and Carl Jung. He was a Christian who also developed a belief in many Gods, giving names to them and drawing their images. They often took the roles of Jung's archetypes, or unconscious patterns from within the human mind that are common to all people. The visions he experienced came to him spontaneously, and much of his poetry was "dictated" from some kind of spiritual realm. His genius was best represented in his ability to create myths. They seemed to function within a Christian framework, as Blake grew up heavily influenced by Swedenborg. The Swedenborgian "new church" was believed to have started in an inner world or "in the heavens" in 1757, the same year that Blake was born. This is a book that outlines Blake's interesting life. Some people thought him to be utterly mad; others considered him a genius. One thing is certain—this biography will not be boring to those interested in the bold adventures of a man who spent his life as a spiritual pioneer. **ISBN 1-58509-225-8 • 384 pages • 6 x 9 • trade paper • $28.95**

***The Divine Pymander: And Other Writings of Hermes Trismegistus*, translated by John D. Chambers.** Within these pages lies a gold mine of wisdom. *The Divine Pymander* may be a strange sounding title, and the attributed author, Hermes Trismegistus, may not have been a single personage, but the information herein is both illuminating and highly relevant. For many centuries these combined works have been known to be highly important on a spiritual level, providing many with an important alternative to standard religious dogma. The teachings are both theological and philosophical, having been often referred to by both the greatest philosophers of Greece and the Church Fathers of Christianity. *The Divine Pymander* was written beyond the time of some of these Greek philosophers, in the first or second century CE, but the later ones gleaned great wisdom from it. It was referred

to by Church Fathers like Tertullian and Justin Martyr—who once stated that if anyone really wanted to learn about God, they should listen to Hermes. Hermes Trismegistus probably lived in Alexandria, and was influenced at least to some degree by Christianity and certain Gnostic ideas. He stressed that when one strives to become free of vice and impurity, a closeness to God may result. Much like the Gnostics, these Hermetic texts considered the body to be in direct conflict with the spirit. The body is something that must be overcome, as it operates on a far lower vibration than spirit and therefore functions as a barrier, separating us from God. Work is required to purify and regenerate the body to bring us closer to God, rather than mere faith. **ISBN 1-58509-046-8 • 196 pages • 6 x 9 • trade paper • $16.95**

Of Heaven and Earth: Essays Presented at the First Sitchin Studies Day, edited by Zecharia Sitchin. ISBN 1-885395-17-5 • 164 pages • 5 1/2 x 8 1/2 • trade paper • illustrated • $14.95

God Games: What Do You Do Forever?, by Neil Freer. ISBN 1-885395-39-6 • 312 pages • 6 x 9 • trade paper • $19.95

Space Travelers and the Genesis of the Human Form: Evidence of Intelligent Contact in the Solar System, by Joan d'Arc. ISBN 1-58509-127-8 • 208 pages • 6 x 9 • trade paper • illustrated • $18.95

Humanity's Extraterrestrial Origins: ET Influences on Humankind's Biological and Cultural Evolution, by Dr. Arthur David Horn with Lynette Mallory-Horn. ISBN 3-931652-31-9 • 373 pages • 6 x 9 • trade paper • $17.00

Past Shock: The Origin of Religion and Its Impact on the Human Soul, by Jack Barranger. ISBN 1-885395-08-6 • 126 pages • 6 x 9 • trade paper • illustrated • $12.95

Flying Serpents and Dragons: The Story of Mankind's Reptilian Past, by R.A. Boulay. ISBN 1-885395-38-8 • 276 pages • 6 x 9 • trade paper • illustrated • $19.95

Triumph of the Human Spirit: The Greatest Achievements of the Human Soul and How Its Power Can Change Your Life, by Paul Tice. ISBN 1-885395-57-4 • 295 pages • 6 x 9 • trade paper • illustrated • $19.95

Mysteries Explored: The Search for Human Origins, UFOs, and Religious Beginnings, by Jack Barranger and Paul Tice. ISBN 1-58509-101-4 • 104 pages • 6 x 9 • trade paper • $12.95

Mushrooms and Mankind: The Impact of Mushrooms on Human Consciousness and Religion, by James Arthur. ISBN 1-58509-151-0 • 180 pages • 6 x 9 • trade paper • $16.95

Vril or Vital Magnetism, with an Introduction by Paul Tice. ISBN 1-58509-030-1 • 124 pages • 5 1/2 x 8 1/2 • trade paper • $12.95

The Odic Force: Letters on Od and Magnetism, by Karl von Reichenbach. ISBN 1-58509-001-8 • 192 pages • 6 x 9 • trade paper • $15.95

The New Revelation: The Coming of a New Spiritual Paradigm, by Arthur Conan Doyle. ISBN 1-58509-220-7 • 124 pages • 6 x 9 • trade paper • $12.95

The Astral World: Its Scenes, Dwellers, and Phenomena, by Swami Panchadasi. ISBN 1-58509-071-9 • 104 pages • 6 x 9 • trade paper • $11.95

Reason and Belief: The Impact of Scientific Discovery on Religious and Spiritual Faith, by Sir Oliver Lodge. ISBN 1-58509-226-6 • 180 pages • 6 x 9 • trade paper • $17.95

William Blake: A Biography, by Basil De Selincourt. ISBN 1-58509-225-8 • 384 pages • 6 x 9 • trade paper • $28.95

The Divine Pymander: And Other Writings of Hermes Trismegistus, translated by John D. Chambers. ISBN 1-58509-046-8 • 196 pages • 6 x 9 • trade paper • $16.95

Theosophy and The Secret Doctrine, by Harriet L. Henderson. Includes ***H.P. Blavatsky: An Outline of Her Life,*** by Herbert Whyte, ISBN 1-58509-075-1 • 132 pages • 6 x 9 • trade paper • $13.95

The Light of Egypt, Volume One: The Science of the Soul and the Stars, by Thomas H. Burgoyne. ISBN 1-58509-051-4 • 320 pages • 6 x 9 • trade paper • illustrated • $24.95

The Light of Egypt, Volume Two: The Science of the Soul and the Stars, by Thomas H. Burgoyne. ISBN 1-58509-052-2 • 224 pages • 6 x 9 • trade paper • illustrated • $17.95

The Jumping Frog and 18 Other Stories: 19 Unforgettable Mark Twain Stories, by Mark Twain. ISBN 1-58509-200-2 • 128 pages • 6 x 9 • trade paper • $12.95

The Devil's Dictionary: A Guidebook for Cynics, by Ambrose Bierce. ISBN 1-58509-016-6 • 144 pages • 6 x 9 • trade paper • $12.95

The Smoky God: Or The Voyage to the Inner World, by Willis George Emerson. ISBN 1-58509-067-0 • 184 pages • 6 x 9 • trade paper • illustrated • $15.95

A Short History of the World, by H.G. Wells. ISBN 1-58509-211-8 • 320 pages • 6 x 9 • trade paper • $24.95

The Voyages and Discoveries of the Companions of Columbus, by Washington Irving. ISBN 1-58509-500-1 • 352 pages • 6 x 9 • hard cover • $39.95

History of Baalbek, by Michel Alouf. ISBN 1-58509-063-8 • 196 pages • 5 x 8 • trade paper • illustrated • $15.95

Ancient Egyptian Masonry: The Building Craft, by Sommers Clarke and R. Engelback. ISBN 1-58509-059-X • 350 pages • 6 x 9 • trade paper • illustrated • $26.95

That Old Time Religion: The Story of Religious Foundations, by Jordan Maxwell and Paul Tice. ISBN 1-58509-100-6 • 220 pages • 6 x 9 • trade paper • $19.95

Jumpin' Jehovah: Exposing the Atrocities of the Old Testament God, by Paul Tice. ISBN 1-58509-102-2 • 104 pages • 6 x 9 • trade paper • $12.95

The Book of Enoch: A Work of Visionary Revelation and Prophecy, Revealing Divine Secrets and Fantastic Information about Creation, Salvation, Heaven and Hell, translated by R. H. Charles. ISBN 1-58509-019-0 • 152 pages • 5 1/2 x 8 1/2 • trade paper • $13.95

The Book of Enoch: Translated from the Editor's Ethiopic Text and Edited with an Enlarged Introduction, Notes and Indexes, Together with a Reprint of the Greek Fragments, edited by R. H. Charles. ISBN 1-58509-080-8 • 448 pages • 6 x 9 • trade paper • $34.95

The Book of the Secrets of Enoch, translated from the Slavonic by W. R. Morfill. Edited, with Introduction and Notes by R. H. Charles. ISBN 1-58509-020-4 • 148 pages • 5 1/2 x 8 1/2 • trade paper • $13.95

Enuma Elish: The Seven Tablets of Creation, Volume One, by L. W. King. ISBN 1-58509-041-7 • 236 pages • 6 x 9 • trade paper • illustrated • $18.95

Enuma Elish: The Seven Tablets of Creation, Volume Two, by L. W. King. ISBN 1-58509-042-5 • 260 pages • 6 x 9 • trade paper • illustrated • $19.95

Enuma Elish, Volumes One and Two: The Seven Tablets of Creation, by L. W. King. Two volumes from above bound as one. ISBN 1-58509-043-3 • 496 pages • 6 x 9 • trade paper • illustrated • $38.90

The Archko Volume: Documents that Claim Proof to the Life, Death, and Resurrection of Christ, by Drs. McIntosh and Twyman. ISBN 1-58509-082-4 • 248 pages • 6 x 9 • trade paper • $20.95

The Lost Language of Symbolism: An Inquiry into the Origin of Certain Letters, Words, Names, Fairy-Tales, Folklore, and Mythologies, by Harold Bayley. ISBN 1-58509-070-0 • 384 pages • 6 x 9 • trade paper • $27.95

The Book of Jasher: A Suppressed Book that was Removed from the Bible, Referred to in Joshua and Second Samuel, translated by Albinus Alcuin (800 AD). ISBN 1-58509-081-6 • 304 pages • 6 x 9 • trade paper • $24.95

The Bible's Most Embarrassing Moments, with an Introduction by Paul Tice. ISBN 1-58509-025-5 • 172 pages • 5 x 8 • trade paper • $14.95

History of the Cross: The Pagan Origin and Idolatrous Adoption and Worship of the Image, by Henry Dana Ward. ISBN 1-58509-056-5 • 104 pages • 6 x 9 • trade paper • illustrated • $11.95

Was Jesus Influenced by Buddhism? A Comparative Study of the Lives and Thoughts of Gautama and Jesus, by Dwight Goddard. ISBN 1-58509-027-1 • 252 pages • 6 x 9 • trade paper • $19.95

History of the Christian Religion to the Year Two Hundred, by Charles B. Waite. ISBN 1-885395-15-9 • 556 pages. • 6 x 9 • hard cover • $25.00

Symbols, Sex, and the Stars, by Ernest Busenbark. ISBN 1-885395-19-1 • 396 pages • 5 1/2 x 8 1/2 • trade paper • $22.95

History of the First Council of Nice: A World's Christian Convention, A.D. 325, by Dean Dudley. ISBN 1-58509-023-9 • 132 pages • 5 1/2 x 8 1/2 • trade paper • $12.95

The World's Sixteen Crucified Saviors, by Kersey Graves. ISBN 1-58509-018-2 • 436 pages • 5 1/2 x 8 1/2 • trade paper • $29.95

Babylonian Influence on the Bible and Popular Beliefs: A Comparative Study of Genesis I.2, by A. Smythe Palmer. ISBN 1-58509-000-X • 124 pages • 6 x 9 • trade paper • $12.95

Biography of Satan: Exposing the Origins of the Devil, by Kersey Graves. ISBN 1-885395-11-6 • 168 pages • 5 1/2 x 8 1/2 • trade paper • $13.95

The Malleus Maleficarum: The Notorious Handbook Once Used to Condemn and Punish "Witches", by Heinrich Kramer and James Sprenger. ISBN 1-58509-098-0 • 332 pages • 6 x 9 • trade paper • $25.95

Crux Ansata: An Indictment of the Roman Catholic Church, by H. G. Wells. ISBN 1-58509-210-X • 160 pages • 6 x 9 • trade paper • $14.95

Emanuel Swedenborg: The Spiritual Columbus, by U.S.E. (William Spear). ISBN 1-58509-096-4 • 208 pages • 6 x 9 • trade paper • $17.95

Dragons and Dragon Lore, by Ernest Ingersoll. ISBN 1-58509-021-2 • 228 pages • 6 x 9 • trade paper • illustrated • $17.95

The Vision of God, by Nicholas of Cusa. ISBN 1-58509-004-2 • 160 pages • 5 x 8 • trade paper • $13.95

The Historical Jesus and the Mythical Christ: Separating Fact From Fiction, by Gerald Massey. ISBN 1-58509-073-5 • 244 pages • 6 x 9 • trade paper • $18.95

Gog and Magog: The Giants in Guildhall; Their Real and Legendary History, with an Account of Other Giants at Home and Abroad, by F.W. Fairholt. ISBN 1-58509-084-0 • 172 pages • 6 x 9 • trade paper • $16.95

The Origin and Evolution of Religion, by Albert Churchward. ISBN 1-58509-078-6 • 504 pages • 6 x 9 • trade paper • $39.95

The Origin of Biblical Traditions, by Albert T. Clay. ISBN 1-58509-065-4 • 220 pages • 5 1/2 x 8 1/2 • trade paper • $17.95

Aryan Sun Myths, by Sarah Elizabeth Titcomb, Introduction by Charles Morris. ISBN 1-58509-069-7 • 192 pages • 6 x 9 • trade paper • $15.95

The Social Record of Christianity, by Joseph McCabe. Includes *The Lies and Fallacies of the Encyclopedia Britannica,* ISBN 1-58509-215-0 • 204 pages • 6 x 9 • trade paper • $17.95

The History of the Christian Religion and Church During the First Three Centuries, by Dr. Augustus Neander. ISBN 1-58509-077-8 • 112 pages • 6 x 9 • trade paper • $12.95

Ancient Symbol Worship: Influence of the Phallic Idea in the Religions of Antiquity, by Hodder M. Westropp and C. Staniland Wake. ISBN 1-58509-048-4 • 120 pages • 6 x 9 • trade paper • illustrated • $12.95

The Gnosis: Or Ancient Wisdom in the Christian Scriptures, by William Kingsland. ISBN 1-58509-047-6 • 232 pages • 6 x 9 • trade paper • $18.95

The Evolution of the Idea of God: An Inquiry into the Origin of Religions, by Grant Allen. ISBN 1-58509-074-3 • 160 pages • 6 x 9 • trade paper • $14.95

Sun Lore of All Ages: A Survey of Solar Mythology, Folklore, Customs, Worship, Festivals, and Superstition, by William Tyler Olcott. ISBN 1-58509-044-1 • 316 pages • 6 x 9 • trade paper • $24.95

Nature Worship: An Account of Phallic Faiths and Practices Ancient and Modern, by the Author of Phallicism with an Introduction by Tedd St. Rain. ISBN 1-58509-049-2 • 112 pages • 6 x 9 • trade paper • illustrated • $12.95

Life and Religion, by Max Muller. ISBN 1-885395-10-8 • 237 pages • 5 1/2 x 8 1/2 • trade paper • $14.95

Jesus: God, Man, or Myth? An Examination of the Evidence, by Herbert Cutner. ISBN 1-58509-072-7 • 304 pages • 6 x 9 • trade paper • $23.95

Pagan and Christian Creeds: Their Origin and Meaning, by Edward Carpenter. ISBN 1-58509-024-7 • 316 pages • 5 1/2 x 8 1/2 • trade paper • $24.95

The Christ Myth: A Study, by Elizabeth Evans. ISBN 1-58509-037-9 • 136 pages • 6 x 9 • trade paper • $13.95

Popery: Foe of the Church and the Republic, by Joseph F. Van Dyke. ISBN 1-58509-058-1 • 336 pages • 6 x 9 • trade paper • illustrated • $25.95

Career of Religious Ideas, by Hudson Tuttle. ISBN 1-58509-066-2 • 172 pages • 5 x 8 • trade paper • $15.95

Buddhist Suttas: Major Scriptural Writings from Early Buddhism, by T.W. Rhys Davids. ISBN 1-58509-079-4 • 376 pages • 6 x 9 • trade paper • $27.95

Early Buddhism, by T. W. Rhys Davids. Includes *Buddhist Ethics: The Way to Salvation?,* by Paul Tice. ISBN 1-58509-076-X • 112 pages • 6 x 9 • trade paper • $12.95

The Fountain-Head of Religion: A Comparative Study of the Principal Religions of the World and a Manifestation of their Common Origin from the Vedas, by Ganga Prasad. ISBN 1-58509-054-9 • 276 pages • 6 x 9 • trade paper • $22.95

India: What Can It Teach Us?, by Max Muller. ISBN 1-58509-064-6 • 284 pages • 5 1/2 x 8 1/2 • trade paper • $22.95

Matrix of Power: How the World has Been Controlled by Powerful People Without Your Knowledge, by Jordan Maxwell. ISBN 1-58509-120-0 • 104 pages • 6 x 9 • trade paper • $12.95

Cyberculture Counterconspiracy: A Steamshovel Web Reader, Volume One, edited by Kenn Thomas. ISBN 1-58509-125-1 • 180 pages • 6 x 9 • trade paper • illustrated • $16.95

Cyberculture Counterconspiracy: A Steamshovel Web Reader, Volume Two, edited by Kenn Thomas. ISBN 1-58509-126-X • 132 pages • 6 x 9 • trade paper • illustrated • $13.95

Oklahoma City Bombing: The Suppressed Truth, by Jon Rappoport. ISBN 1-885395-22-1 • 112 pages • 5 1/2 x 8 1/2 • trade paper • $12.95

The Protocols of the Learned Elders of Zion, by Victor Marsden. ISBN 1-58509-015-8 • 312 pages • 6 x 9 • trade paper • $24.95

Secret Societies and Subversive Movements, by Nesta H. Webster. ISBN 1-58509-092-1 • 432 pages • 6 x 9 • trade paper • $29.95

The Secret Doctrine of the Rosicrucians, by Magus Incognito. ISBN 1-58509-091-3 • 256 pages • 6 x 9 • trade paper • $20.95

The Origin and Evolution of Freemasonry: Connected with the Origin and Evolution of the Human Race, by Albert Churchward. ISBN 1-58509-029-8 • 240 pages • 6 x 9 • trade paper • $18.95

The Lost Key: An Explanation and Application of Masonic Symbols, by Prentiss Tucker. ISBN 1-58509-050-6 • 192 pages • 6 x 9 • trade paper • illustrated • $15.95

The Character, Claims, and Practical Workings of Freemasonry, by Rev. C.G. Finney. ISBN 1-58509-094-8 • 288 pages • 6 x 9 • trade paper • $22.95

The Secret World Government or "The Hidden Hand": The Unrevealed in History, by Maj.-Gen., Count Cherep-Spiridovich. ISBN 1-58509-093-X • 270 pages • 6 x 9 • trade paper • $21.95

The Magus, Book One: A Complete System of Occult Philosophy, by Francis Barrett. ISBN 1-58509-031-X • 200 pages • 6 x 9 • trade paper • illustrated • $16.95

The Magus, Book Two: A Complete System of Occult Philosophy, by Francis Barrett. ISBN 1-58509-032-8 • 220 pages • 6 x 9 • trade paper • illustrated • $17.95

The Magus, Book One and Two: A Complete System of Occult Philosophy, by Francis Barrett. ISBN 1-58509-033-6 • 420 pages • 6 x 9 • trade paper • illustrated • $34.90

The Key of Solomon The King, by S. Liddell MacGregor Mathers. ISBN 1-58509-022-0 • 152 pages • 6 x 9 • trade paper • illustrated • $12.95

Magic and Mystery in Tibet, by Alexandra David-Neel. ISBN 1-58509-097-2 • 352 pages • 6 x 9 • trade paper • $26.95

The Comte de St. Germain, by I. Cooper Oakley. ISBN 1-58509-068-9 • 280 pages • 6 x 9 • trade paper • illustrated • $22.95

Alchemy Rediscovered and Restored, by A. Cockren. ISBN 1-58509-028-X • 156 pages • 5 1/2 x 8 1/2 • trade paper • $13.95

The 6th and 7th Books of Moses, with an Introduction by Paul Tice. ISBN 1-58509-045-X • 188 pages • 6 x 9 • trade paper • illustrated • $16.95